WHIZ-BANG
WONDERS
From the **GOOD OLD DAYS™**

Edited by Ken and Janice Tate

HOUSE of
WHITE
BIRCHES

PUBLISHERS
SINCE 1947

Whiz-Bang Wonders From the Good Old Days™

Editors: Ken and Janice Tate
Managing Editor: Barb Sprunger
Editorial Assistant: Joanne Neuenschwander
Copy Supervisor: Michelle Beck
Copy Editors: Nicki Lehman, Beverly Richardson, Läna Schurb
Assistant Editors: Marla Freeman, Marj Morgan, June Sprunger

Publishing Services Manager: Brenda Gallmeyer
Art Director: Brad Snow
Assistant Art Director: Nick Pierce
Graphic Arts Supervisor: Ronda Bechinski
Production Artists: Erin Augsburger, Janice Tate
Traffic Coordinator: Sandra Beres
Production Assistants: Cheryl Kempf, Jessica Tate
Photography: Justin P. Wiard, Kelly Wiard

Chief Executive Officer: John Robinson
Publishing Director: David McKee
Marketing Director: Dan Fink
Editorial Director: Vivian Rothe

Printed in the United States of America
First Printing: 2005
Library of Congress Number: 2004117380
ISBN: 1-59217-080-3
Good Old Days Customer Service: (800) 829-5865

Every effort has been made to ensure the accuracy of the material in this book.
However, the publisher is not responsible for research errors or typographical mistakes in this publication.

We would like to thank Curtis Publishing for the art prints used in this book.

For fine-art prints and more information on the artists featured in *Whiz-Bang Wonders From the Good Old Days*, contact:

Curtis Publishing, Indianapolis, IN 46202, (317) 633-2070, www.curtispublishing.com

1 2 3 4 5 6 7 8 9

*D*ear Friends of the Good Old Days,

When my wife, Janice, and I started work on the concept for this book, we wanted to take a look back at the days when so much was changing in our country and our world. The Baby Boom years following World War II and through the 1950s was an exciting time to be alive. Technological advances changed almost every aspect of our lives—and most of those changes were for the good.

We have seen lots of "retro" books, and most treat the 1940s and 1950s with irreverence. Those fun, wide-eyed, innocent years are generally jokingly poked at as being campy, naive and downright silly. Janice and I wanted none of that, so we decided to take a "retro with respect" approach to the era.

As we considered what to call the book, we settled on *Whiz-Bang Wonders* because in those days it was popular to refer to any great idea as being "whiz-bang."

Actually, it was an appropriate term. The original "whiz-bang" was an artillery shell from World War I that you couldn't hear until just before it exploded. It was said that all you hear was a *whiz* and then *bang*!

That was how things seemed to happen in the 1950s. Changes came so rapidly that we barely had time to adapt before the next whiz-bang wonder was on our doorstep.

The changes were profound and were most notable within the walls of our homes. From the front room to the back yard, from the kitchen to the playroom—everything we did seemed new, different, better and more exciting.

We have tried to capture the wide-eyed wonder of those days within the pages of this special book. Whether you were a Baby Boom parent or child, Janice and I hope you enjoy this look back at those Whiz-Bang Wonders from the Good Old Days!

Ken Tate

❧ Contents ❧

Living Room Wonders • 6

Mealtime Miracles • 34

Mother's Little Helpers • 62

Fads & Fantasies • 82

Permanent Solutions • 102

The Necessary Room • 122

The Great Outdoors • 142

JOHN FALTER

Living Room Wonders

Chapter One

*I*t was late afternoon, and a stagecoach was being robbed on the high plains. The marshal was pinned down behind an abutment of rocks, with the bandit blazing bullets at every movement. The lawman distracted the robber by raising his hat above the crest of the bluff, while warily sneaking his six-shooter unseen around the edge of the rocks.

Bang! Bang! Our son shot the bad guy, saved the stagecoach from imminent danger, and good won out over evil again—all while I peacefully rested on the living room couch.

Such were the battles waged after the little screen found its way into our living rooms and our hearts. Riding with Roy Rogers or the Lone Ranger, flying with Sky King or just hanging around the apartment with Lucy and Ricky, our little boy never realized how the living room had changed since his mother and I were his age.

Ah, the wonders of the modern living room! Plush carpets, comfortable chairs, thermostatically controlled heat and even air conditioning made the parlors and front rooms of the 1950s much more accommodating for those of us living in the whiz-bang era.

But the centerpiece of the new living room had to be the television. The old Philco radio was no longer the focal point as it had been for most American families in the 1930s and '40s.

Now the family gathered around the television after supper, reveling in the new technology even when the picture was snowy and the programming was limited. Why, looking at the TV station's test pattern was better than no TV at all! Just ask our son.

In this chapter we'll remember a few of the living room wonders that made life warmer, safer, softer and more entertaining back in the Good Old Days.

—Ken Tate

Our First Television

By Terry R. Shaw

Television was still in its infancy—a novelty more than the norm—when I was growing up in the early 1950s. I can't imagine not having a TV today, but there was a time, of course. I grew up in a small town in Minnesota, and this whiz-bang wonder was first mentioned in the local newspaper in August 1948. An article—not an ad—told the public that one of the two local electric appliance stores had a new Motorola television in the store. According to the article, the television "projects a clear image of the radio program"; the newspaper writer predicted that someday, televisions would be as common as radios in homes.

A year later, the other electric store announced in the paper that the store's owner had a new television in his home and people were invited, by appointment, to come and view "this new entertainment."

We got our first television in 1953, when I was in first grade. Before that, I listened to *Arthur Godfrey*, *Gang Busters* and *The Lone Ranger* on the radio on weekdays, and to a kids' show called *The Teddy Bears' Picnic* on Saturday mornings. My mother, who was raising four boys by herself, told us about the new television the night before we got it. I couldn't wait to get home from school the next day. I told all my friends, "We're getting a TV at our house!"

This whiz-bang wonder was first mentioned in the local newspaper in August 1948.

I hardly impressed them, though, as most of them already had had televisions for a couple of years. But it was a big deal for me.

When I got off the bus, ran into the house and saw the television standing against the wall in our living room, it felt like Christmas morning. It had a deep reddish-brown mahogany cabinet about a 36 inches tall and 18 inches wide. Two brass lions' heads holding rings in their mouths decorated the fake doors in the bottom half.

The bottom half of the cabinet served no purpose, as the tiny speaker was right on the top. The top half of the cabinet contained a 12-inch, black-and-white screen. Right under the screen, a pull-down door emblazoned with the word "EMERSON" in gold letters concealed the controls.

Mom had bought the television for about $150 from a friend who sold Emersons from his house. On top of the television was a note that read, "Don't touch until I'm home. Mom." Rats! Mom didn't get home until 5 p.m.! When she finally got home, my brothers and I started pestering her to turn it on.

The Edgar Bergens watching the real-as-life performance of Charlie McCarthy on Magnavox Belvedere 20-inch TV.

Magnavox the magnificent gift for all the family

One gift pleases everybody—a magnificent Magnavox! So why not make sure that everyone in your family will be tickled pink with what you give? Why not pool your Christmas spending money and buy one magnificent gift for all—the priceless gift of endless entertainment! Year in, year out your entire family will find your gift a source of daily pleasure and pride...as long as it's a Magnavox. And you, in turn, will find the right price for your budget—and the right cabinet design for your home—among the many superb models offered by Magnavox. Only America's finest stores are selected to sell Magnavox. See your classified telephone directory. The Magnavox Company, Fort Wayne 4, Indiana.

THE BELVEDERE (also shown above). AM-FM radio-phonograph in rich mahogany or blonde oak finish. Add superb Magnavox 20-inch TV now or later.

BETTER SIGHT...BETTER SOUND...BETTER BUY

the magnificent Magnavox television radio-phonograph

Color and Ultra High Frequency Units Readily Attachable

Edgar Bergen and his family watch Charlie McCarthy in this advertisement from 1950. Edgar and Charlie were featured in a television pilot in November 1950, but The Charlie McCarthy Show never made it to the small screen on a regular basis.

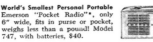

Whiz-Bang TV Firsts

1940

April 16 — First televised baseball game, WGN Chicago

1946

May 9 — First hour-long television entertainment show, NBC's *Hour Glass*

1947

Oct. 13 — *Kukla, Fran & Ollie*, WBKB Chicago

Dec. 27 — *Howdy Doody*

1948

June 8 — *The Milton Berle Show*

June 20 — *Toast of the Town*, CBS; Ed Sullivan is the host.

1949

Jan. 31 — First daytime soap opera, *These Are My Children*

June 27 — *Captain Video and His Video Rangers*

1950

July 23 — *The Gene Autry Show*

Oct. 12 — *The George Burns and Gracie Allen Show*, CBS

1951

June 25 — First commercial color TV program, a four-hour-long *Arthur Godfrey Show*, airs on CBS.

Sept. 30 — *The Red Skelton Show*

Oct. 15 — *I Love Lucy*, CBS

1952

Jan. 3 — *Dragnet* with Jack Webb, NBC

June 19 — *I've Got a Secret*

Oct. 1 — First UHF television station, Portland, Ore.

Dec. 5 — *The Abbott and Costello Show*

1953

Jan. 2 — *The Life of Riley*

Jan. 19 — 68% of sets in the U.S. are tuned to CBS, as Lucy Ricardo of *I Love Lucy* gives birth to a baby boy—just as Lucille Ball actually does in real life.

Sept. 29 — *Make Room for Daddy*

1954

Feb. 1 — *The Secret Storm*, CBS

Mar. 15 — *CBS Morning Show* with Walter Cronkite

Sept. 12 — *Lassie*, CBS

Sept. 27 — *The Tonight Show*, NBC

Oct. 3 — *Father Knows Best*

1955

Jan. 19	*The Millionaire*, CBS
June 7	*The $64,000 Question*, CBS
July 2	*The Lawrence Welk Show*, ABC
Sept. 10	*Gunsmoke*, CBS
Oct. 1	*The Honeymooners*
Oct. 2	*Alfred Hitchcock Presents*
Oct. 3	*Captain Kangaroo*
Oct. 13	*Grand Ole Opry*, ABC

1956

Dec. 28	Last *Ding Dong School*, NBC

1957

Sept. 14	*Have Gun, Will Travel*, CBS
Sept. 21	*Perry Mason*, CBS
Oct. 4	*Leave It to Beaver*, CBS
Oct. 7	*American Bandstand*

1958

July 3	*The Andy Williams Show*, ABC
Sept. 5	*Wanted: Dead or Alive*, CBS; Steve McQueen stars as bounty hunter Josh Randall.
Oct. 2	*The Huckleberry Hound Show*

1959

Jan. 5	Bozo the Clown
Mar. 8	The Marx brothers' final TV appearance together
April 20	Desilu Playhouse on CBS presents a two-part show titled *The Untouchables*, later a weekly series later
Sept. 12	*Bonanza*
Oct. 2	Rod Serling's *Twilight Zone*, CBS

1960

Sept. 29	*My Three Sons*, ABC
Sept. 30	*The Flintstones*
Oct. 3	*The Andy Griffith Show*, CBS

1961

Jan. 30	*Yogi Bear Show* debuts
Sept. 28	*Hazel*, NBC
	Dr. Kildare, NBC
Oct. 2	*Ben Casey*, ABC
Oct. 3	*The Dick Van Dyke Show*

1962

Jan. 6	*Beany and Cecil*
April 16	Walter Cronkite anchors *The CBS Evening News*.
Sept. 26	*The Beverly Hillbillies*, CBS
Oct. 1	Johnny Carson hosts his first *Tonight Show* on NBC.

"We're not turning that TV on until we've eaten supper and all of the dishes are washed and put away," she said.

We rushed through the meal and were extra helpful clearing the kitchen table and washing the dishes. Mom had also insisted that we pray every night while we did the dishes. Our minds already wandered while repeating "Hail, Mary" over and over, but this night the prayers didn't do us a bit of good as we mumbled our responses to Mom's lead as fast as we could.

Finally, just before 7 o'clock, we all gathered in the living room, jockeying for the best place on the sofa, which Mom had pulled to the center of the room, facing the television. The single easy chair off to the side had been declared hers.

She turned off all the lights except for a special "TV lamp" that sat on top of the television. The 40-watt light bulb was enclosed in a red upside-down cone, which was perched on the middle of a little red settee on which sat two miniature plaster Chinese people, a boy and a girl, dressed in red. Mom had been told to have a TV lamp so that her children's eyes wouldn't be ruined by watching television.

The big moment finally had arrived. Mom reached down and turned the volume knob to the right with a click. The screen started to flicker. A small white dot in the center of the screen slowly grew as the picture tube warmed up. This was taking an eternity!

Suddenly the dot jumped to fill the screen. We sat and stared at a full screen of … nothing. Nothing but snow, accompanied by a roaring hiss from the tiny speaker. Mom turned the volume down and then, *clunk, clunk, clunk, clunk,* she turned the channel tuner dial, which had numbers from 1 to 12 on it, until she came to a channel that wasn't all snow. Somewhere in there was the faint image of *The Goodyear TV Playhouse,* an hour-long drama without cowboys or police shooting at bad guys. We had waited for *this?*

"Mom, isn't there anything else on?" I pleaded. I had heard about cowboy shows like *Gunsmoke,* police dramas like *Dragnet,* comedies like *I Love Lucy* and *The Jack Benny Show. Clunk, clunk, clunk, clunk* … She turned the dial. "I'm sorry, boys," she said. "That's all I can find. Just this one channel comes in."

"Why didn't you buy a better TV?" I cried.

"It's not the TV," my older brother said to me. "It's the antenna, dope." My brother knew about these things.

"Mom, we need a better antenna."

"Well, we'll just have to do with this for now," Mom said, with finality.

We sat through the drama, bored to tears.

Over the next few days, we did everything we could to improve the reception, including moving the TV set closer to the window, but all we could get were four snowy channels from Minneapolis and St. Paul, 60 miles east of us.

Mom called her friend who had sold her the television. He came over and went up to the roof. He yelled down, "Is it clearer yet?" over and over until Mom finally said, "Well, that's the best we're gonna get it, I suppose."

Our town was just too far from the transmitting towers in the Twin Cities.

It didn't get any better until a few years later, when the stations started building bigger transmitters.

Television shows didn't come on until 6 a.m. Before that, all you got was a test pattern. Then, at midnight, everything went off after the national anthem was played with the movie of jets flying in front of the American flag. Then the test pattern was the only thing on until morning.

I suppose you could use it to adjust your contrast, brightness, vertical and horizontal hold. Those were the four control knobs, along with the volume/on-and-off knob.

We'd be watching a TV show and suddenly the picture would start twisting. One of us would have to jump up, run to the set and delicately turn the appropriate knob until the picture straightened out. I sat on the floor right up by the screen because I couldn't see the television very well. Mom kept telling me to back up from the screen because I was going to ruin my eyes, but I would just inch forward back to where I had been. So I became the official knob turner. I became quite good at keeping a nice, straight picture for my family. Plus, I got to "surf" the channels after shows ended.

"There … leave that on!"

"No, we ain't watchin' that junk!"

"Mom, make him put it back where it was!"

One clever television show that was on Saturday mornings from 1953–1957 was called *Winky Dink and You.* It featured the adventures of Winky Dink, a star-headed cartoon boy, and his dog, Woofer. Jack Barry hosted it.

There were a lot of cartoon TV shows on the air in the 1950s, but *Winky Dink* was different. Jack Barry wore a plain suit—and the show was interactive. For 50 cents, I sent away for a light green plastic Winky Dink screen and a "magic" black crayon. When I put the Winky Dink

Kukla, Fran and Ollie started out as a program for youngsters, but quickly became a favorite for everyone. This ad from January 1951 featured a family enjoying the Kuklapolitans on their new television.

screen on our TV screen and wiped it with a cloth, it "magically" stuck.

Winky Dink always got himself into jams in the cartoons and ended up being chased by some villain. Suddenly he would find himself at the edge of a cliff. Then the cartoon world freeze and Jack Barry's voice would give us instructions. "Quick, kids, connect the dots and draw a bridge for Winky Dink!"

I'd grab my magic crayon, draw the bridge, and Winky Dink would run across it. Then I'd quickly erase the bridge, as instructed by Barry, and the villain would be foiled again. I saved Winky Dink's life many times.

At the end of each segment, we were instructed to trace parts of letters at the bottom of the screen so that we could eventually complete and read a secret message at the end of the show. I guess *Winky Dink and You* was the world's first interactive "video game." ❖

The Hillsdale by RCA VICTOR

with Million Proof pictures nearly *twice the size* of this page. Beautiful, Traditional cabinet comes in rich mahogany or walnut finish at the same low price. Limed oak finish slightly higher. Model 9T77.

RCA VICTOR

RCA   Division of Radio Corporation of America

Catching the Waves

hile television was taking over in living rooms of North America, modern times were not just redefining what we saw, but what we heard as well. Catching the waves—sound waves, that is—was a whole new game in the Good Old Days.

For a lot of folks, the venerable radio—not the television—remained the centerpiece of the living room. The golden age of radio was in its heyday in the late 1940s and the early 1950s.

We gathered around our radios' glowing dials as the biggest names and most popular programs in show business joined us in our parlors and living rooms. There were variety shows from the likes of Bob Hope, Bing Crosby and Fred Allen. Comedies from the "ands": Fibber McGee and Molly, Lum 'n' Abner, George and Gracie. Thrillers like *The Shadow, Inner Sanctum* and *The Green Hornet.* Westerns, detective shows, romances—all continued to entertain us as the TV phenomenon was getting off the ground.

But the face of radio was changing. First came the advent of FM (frequency modulation). Its clear signal had been tested in the early 1930s by Edwin Armstrong, the father of FM radio, but there were still only 40 FM stations in 1939.

That changed with the proliferation of FM stations in the 1940s. General Electric was the moving force behind the FM wave. Stars of radio and Hollywood like the lovely Virginia Mayo (who died Jan. 17, 2005, at the age of 84) were tapped to tout the "natural color" of the sound coming from the GE radios.

Then came the miracles of modern technology that took the large cabinet models and gave us the wonderful world of miniaturization.

Self-charging portable—No more battery worries. Renews its power over and over again. Brings in more stations and has finer tone than many consoles. Light weight, cast aluminum case. See Model 250.

Surprising tone-performance-value—All these are yours in Model 200. Razor sharp tuning. Easy to read airplane type dial. This radio's rosewood brown plastic cabinet typifies the best in modern design.

General Electric's finest table radio-phonograph—Revel in Model 303's glorious natural color tone! Discover new beauty in your favorite records when played by the amazing G-E Electronic Reproducer.

GENERAL ELECTRIC FM *It's wonderful...*

You'll hear the full glory of natural color tone in this great new radio-phonograph

Lovely VIRGINIA MAYO, currently featured in the Samuel Goldwyn production, "THE BEST YEARS OF OUR LIVES."

Exciting as a first night on Broadway—thrilling as a Hollywood premiere—is your first hearing of this entirely different, magnificently finer kind of radio.

At last electronic science triumphs over radio's old foes: static, fading and station interference. Through the magic of FM (genuine Armstrong FM), you revel in the glory of natural color tone heard against a background of velvety silence.

In recordings, too, these triumphant new instruments reveal beauty never heard before, as the exclusive new G-E Electronic Reproducer faithfully recreates the delicate shadings—brings you all the music on your records. There's a new thrill waiting at your General Electric dealer's. Ask him for a demonstration—today.

GENERAL ⊛ ELECTRIC
170-F1

LEADER IN RADIO, TELEVISION AND ELECTRONICS

RADIOS

Here's the radio-phonograph music lovers have waited for—With wonderful FM (genuine Armstrong FM) and finer reception of standard and shortwave broadcasts. Precision tuning with the G-E Guillotine Tuner. 12" Dynapower Speaker. 9 tubes plus rectifier. Sensational G-E Electronic Reproducer. 18th Century inspired mahogany cabinet. Stores 120 records. Ask for Model 417.

Soon, portables allowed us to take our radios—and our music, news and favorite programs—with us, whether to beach or bedroom. Instead of tubes that took time to warm up, we now had transistors that gave us instant-on sound, plus the innovation of tinier and tinier versions of our old standby from the living room.

Radio wasn't the only medium that had new ways to catch the waves. Recordings were wowing us as well.

The first records were on cylinders and were played on the original invention of Thomas Alva Edison in the late 19th century.

Soon the cylinder disappeared in favor of the 10-inch 78-RPM record, but 78s were apt to break, and the five-minute maximum recording length meant one song per side.

But the venerable 78s remained the industry standard until 1948.

That year, the Columbia studios came out with the 12-inch LP (long-playing) vinyl record. This new format could play 25 minutes per side. The recorded album was born.

Next came a seven-inch, 45-RPM vinyl record developed by RCA Victor. The wave of 45s began in the early 1950s, and came into its own with the age of rock and roll.

Recording stars like Tony Martin lent their voices to 45s and their faces to ads for RCA Victor, assuring young and old alike that the 45 fad was "sweeping the country."

Add to that automatic record changers and high-fidelity sound, and it is no wonder that sock-hops and slumber parties would never be the same again.

Catching the waves in brand-new ways was definitely catching on in the Good Old Days. ❖

ACTUAL SIZE
New Bulova "Viceroy" all-Transistor plug-in clock radio. Plays instantly without warm-up. Amazingly clear, rich tone. Wakes you gently to music. Ebony, ivory, blue, $39.95†. *Also available:* Bulova "Performer". Slide-rule tuning. Full-feature clock wakes you to music or alarm $49.95†

Left: The age of smaller and smaller circuitry pulled radios from our living rooms. The new technology brought us whiz-bang advances like clock radios and portable phonographs for our bedrooms and transistor radios for our pockets. This Bulova advertisement was published in May 1963. Facing page: RCA Victor ad published in April 1950.

"*Finest tone quality I've ever heard*"

"The '45' is what musicians and music lovers have been waiting for—recorded music that sounds better, plays 'easier,' costs less." *says Tony Martin*

It's Sweeping the country

RCA Victor "45"

Victrola "45"—a complete automatic phonograph, not an attachment—requires less than half the space of an ordinary phonograph. AC. RCA Victor 45EY. **$29.95**

Add the "45" to your present set—radio, phono, or television—with this automatic record changer attachment. AC. **$12.95**

Here's the "45" plus AM radio in a maroon plastic cabinet less than one cubic foot in size. AC. RCA Victor 9Y51. **$59.95**

Stunning new console has the "45" changer, a separate automatic changer for 78 and 33⅓ records, plus AM FM radio. Big 12-inch speaker. Choice of finishes. RCA Victor A78. **$199.95**

Never in the history of the record industry has a new development moved ahead so fast in so short a time. The "45" now outsells any other system . . . 65,000 automatic record changers a month and more than two million records a MONTH!

Sounds Better Critics call "45" tone superior . . . the stars say it's a musician's dream of hearing his music perfectly reproduced.

Plays Easier Even a 4-year-old can pile up to 10 of the non-breakable 7-inch records on the big center spindle—then press one button once for up to 50 minutes of music.

Costs Less The "45" is the *least expensive* automatic record changer as well as the

simplest, surest and finest ever. Red Seal records 95¢, Bluebirds 46¢, others 65¢.

You can get the "45" alone, with radio, or in luxuriously complete television combinations. See it, hear it, play it yourself—today. It's the record-playing system of the future.

Already over 2000 "45" record titles. Among them, 15 great new albums of all-time hits, specially arranged for dancing, and played by big-name bands.

Prices shown are suggested list prices and are subject to change without notice. Slightly higher in the far West and South. Record prices do not include excise tax.

"Victrola"—T. M. Reg. U.S. Pat. Off.

WORLD LEADER IN RADIO...FIRST IN RECORDED MUSIC...FIRST IN TELEVISION *RCA Victor* Division of Radio Corporation of America

Wonderful Relaxation

The whiz-bang years meant that the living room became a peaceful harbor for hardworking men and women. The transformation began with the furniture in which we relaxed.

The recliner became a fixture almost indelibly tied to the living room, the television and the remote control.

For nearly a hundred years, researchers had noted the natural tendency of American men to tilt their chairs back and put up their feet, whether on porch railing, table or mantelpiece.

Then, in 1928, two cousins, Ed Shoemaker and Ed Knabusch, from Monroe, Mich., patented a new chair made from hardwood slats that was the first recliner. It was far from the

comfortable seat it is today, and some vendors refused to market what could easily be described as a very expensive deck chair. The next year, on advice from one of their potential customers, the cousins upholstered the frame of their invention, and they soon could not keep up with demand. The La-Z-Boy recliner was born.

By the mid- to late 1950s, recliners were ubiquitous in American homes. Several other companies, including BarcaLounger, were jumping into the recliner market.

In 1955, BarcaLounger was trying to convince Christmas shoppers that "Every Santa wants a BarcaLounger." Indeed, the recliner went to the top of the list for many husbands and fathers.

The recliner wasn't the only living room wonder in the Good Old Days. The sofa was

YOU HAVE TO SEE IT TO BELIEVE IT!

FLASH-MATIC TUNING BY ZENITH

ONLY ZENITH HAS IT!

A flash of magic light from across the room (no wires, no cords) turns set _on_, _off_, or _changes channels_...and you remain in your easy chair!

With a beam of magic light

this Zenith "flash tuner" works TV miracles! Absolutely harmless to humans!

Remember when the "remote control" was one of the kids? Zenith brought us the corded "Lazy Bones" remote control in 1950 (inset, right), and then the "Flash-Matic" wireless remote control in 1955. That control had its limitations, however. If the front of the TV was in direct sunlight, the tuner sometimes started rotating through channels.

bringing something new to homes as well.

In 1940, the Simmons company introduced the Hide-A-Bed sofa (which grew out of the concept of the studio couch of the 1930s). The pull-out bed gave us a way to keep visiting family and friends off the hard, cold floor.

The fold-out couch was notoriously uncomfortable—and the butt of many jokes on later TV sitcoms.

The Hide-A-Bed also gave studio apartments a new lease on life by providing a comfortable sleeping arrangement while preserving space. ❖

Letting Our Fingers Do the Walking

A t first telephones were cumbersome, bulky devices on the living room wall. Like Henry Ford's cars, you could get them in any color you wanted—as long as the color you wanted was black.

Then came the advent of the rotary-dial desktop telephone of the 1950s. Not only were the new phones smaller, but hard plastic casings burst into living rooms with designer colors to fit any modern decor.

Remember party lines? Burgeoning use of phones in the 1950s and 1960s spelled doom for them except in rural areas. We became so accustomed to telephones that multi-phone homes were inevitable. It became fashionable to have a telephone with a long, coiled cord in the kitchen, where suppertime calls were more welcome than in today's telemarketing world.

Long-distance rates declined even as families spread out, making it easier to stay in touch. "You should see my cast!" one granddaughter exclaimed to grandparents half a nation away. Most grandparents would agree that it was easier to hear about the broken arm "from the horse's mouth" than to read about it in a letter. ❖

Whiz-Bang Facts

The first transcontinental microwave system began operating on Aug. 17, 1951. The Bell Telephone System built 107 relay stations spaced about 30 miles apart to form a wireless link from New York to San Francisco. It cost the Bell System about $40 million.

～

Wichita Falls, Texas, became the first American city to institute all-number calling (ANC) in January 1958.

For the first time, callers dialed seven numbers without letters or names. Until then, exchanges had used a system of letters, names and numbers developed 40 years earlier.

It took about 15 years for ANC to be used universally. Only then did numbers like LAkeside 2-1057 disappear.

～

The Ansafone, created by inventor Dr. Kazuo Hashimoto for the Phonetel company, was the first answering machine sold in the United States, beginning in 1960.

～

Teri Pall invented the first cordless telephone in 1965.

～

The emergency number 911 was set aside for use nationwide by AT&T in 1968.

"Let your fingers do the walking" was a slogan coined for a Yellow Pages advertising campaign that began in 1970.

WALL TELEPHONE: in rich ivory or black. Because it takes up no working space, it's the ideal additional telephone for kitchen, workshop, rumpus room, or elsewhere.

LIGHT-UP DIAL TELEPHONE: the dial is illuminated as soon as the handset is picked up. Easy to dial in dark or dimly lit rooms — bedrooms, nurseries, sickrooms.

VOLUME CONTROL TELEPHONE: button control enables user to increase sound volume as required for best individual results. A boon for people with impaired hearing.

PLUG-IN TELEPHONE: portable extension plugs into telephone outlets as additional telephone for occasional use. Also permanent extensions wherever you wish.

TELEPHONE ANSWERING SET: automatically answers calls when you're out, gives callers a recorded message and lets them leave a half-minute recorded message for you.

Number, Please

By Shelia W. Coker

*I*f you've never experienced rural party-line phone service, you probably don't realize what a wonder rotary dialing was. In the days before dial phones, when you picked up your receiver, you would hear a lady say, "Number, please." You would tell her what phone number you wanted to reach, or the name of the person you were calling, and she would make the connection for you.

In our area, the machinery that made all this possible was the switchboard that sat in my grandmother's front room. But another piece of "equipment" that was just as important was her memory. She *was* the telephone service for more than 40 years in Caneyville, a small, rural community in Grayson County, Ky.

Between 1920–1963, my grandparents' house was visited by everyone in town at one time or another, including the occasional late-night visitor. There were no "pay phones" then, but there was a blue-and-white metal sign on a telephone pole at the end of their driveway that read "Public Telephone." The wall-mounted phone with a cloth-wrapped cord was housed in an oak box.

In the 1920s, when telephone service was new to rural areas, my grandmother operated the switchboard, sent out the monthly bills, and personally visited each customer's house or business to collect payments to send to the phone company. If anyone needed to make a long-distance call, she would contact the operator in Louisville who would make the connection. My grandmother would get the time and charges for the call from the Louisville operator and the caller would pay her when the call was finished. Grandmother kept a log of all long-distance calls, and the time and charges for each one.

My grandparents' house was next to the only grocery store in town, and Saturday was always a busy day. People came into town to shop at the feed store and the grocery, buy gasoline and perhaps eat lunch. Beginning in the 1930s, when customers were responsible for getting their telephone bill payments to my grandmother, they often came to her house, too.

They were often greeted by my grandfather, who sat on the retaining wall in front of the house. He talked to everyone who came by while he whittled on a cedar stick. In the early 1950s, customers might also encounter a small girl sitting in the porch swing, playing with her dolls.

All this activity made my life interesting, for I spent summers with my grandparents until 1964. From the time I was about 10 years old, I was sent to the post office about two blocks away twice a day to pick up the mail. (There was no mail delivery in our town.) I was also sent to the bank each day, carrying the deposit in an important-looking cloth bag with a big zipper across the top of it. Everyone knew who I was and what was in that bag, but no one ever bothered me.

My grandparents slept on a roll-away bed in the middle of the front room so she could respond to the night alarm if someone decided to make a call. It was not unusual for someone to come to the front door in the middle of the night to use the "public telephone," especially if the weather was bad.

During the summer, my grandmother would be washing supper dishes around 5:30 p.m. If anyone tried to make a call then, I might answer the switchboard. I knew what to do, but I didn't know all the names and the number of rings for each person on a party line. I would call out the name to Grandmother and she would tell me without hesitation.

On summer evenings, townspeople sometimes dropped by for a visit. They sat in the front room with my grandmother or in the swing on the porch. They could visit with her from there, chatting through the big window that was behind the swing and next to the switchboard.

My grandfather was a section hand on the Illinois Central Railroad. Though he had a car, he always walked to work. He became hard of hearing later in life and almost shouted when he answered the switchboard.

Below: The Caneyville, Ky., "telephone exchange"—my grandparents' front room—in the early 1950s. Seated is Ruby Minton; my grandmother, Goldia Warfield, is standing.

Christmas was always wonderful. People used to bring my grandparents all sorts of things, especially homemade cakes and candy. I think they really appreciated the fact that phone service was always available, no matter what.

My grandmother hired a lady to work at the switchboard from 8 a.m.–5 p.m. Monday through Friday, and from 12 noon–5 p.m. on Sundays so that she could get her own house-work and laundry done.

We used to take a drive every Sunday after-noon, weather permitting. That's about the only time my grandfather's car was ever out of the garage. My mother also worked days at the switchboard while my father was overseas dur-ing World War II.

One of the small duties associated with that switchboard involved a single switch in the upper left corner. Each day at noon, Grandmoth-er turned it to blow the whistle at the firehouse. That was a big deal when I was 5.

As people talked to the operator while mak-ing their calls, a lot of community information (and gossip) came into our possession. Our little town did not have a newspaper, and the paper produced in the county seat was pub-lished only once a week. So a lot of legitimate information was spread via the "telephone exchange" office.

The first weekend in October, the local school fair was the place to be. There were drawings for prizes like quilts and cakes, jig-dancing and hog-calling contests, lots of hand-made items for sale, and snack bars. A queen was even crowned! It was a lot of fun and nearly everyone attended. We took turns man-ning the switchboard so that everyone in the family could go.

In later years, whenever I watched *The Andy Griffith Show* and the characters picked up the phone and talked to the operator, I thought about that apparatus in my grandmother's house.

She was 94 when she passed away in December 1998. During her last two years, even when she couldn't remember that I was her granddaughter, she could still tell me exact information about names, phone numbers and the telephone business from those early days. ❖

The Old Party Line

By Carol Sue Brodbeck

Our first phone was an oak box that hung on the kitchen wall. On the left was the earpiece on a cord that was held up to the caller's ear. The mouthpiece extended from the middle of the box. On the right was a crank used to ring up the party we were calling. A partial turn created a short ring; turning it farther created a longer ring.

Ours was an eight-party line and each family had its own sequence of long and short rings. We only answered when we heard our special ring. We knew of one party, however, who picked up on every-one's calls. It was the best way for her to find out what was happening. When we heard the fire call, everyone picked up to find out where to go to help fight the fire.

To reach the operator, we just turned the crank on the right side of the phone to make one long ring. She then connected us to whatever number we needed.

Children were not allowed to play on the phone. One day, though, I was alone and I was curious about what that thing really was. I pulled the big kitchen chair over to the phone and climbed up. I did exactly what I had seen my parents do: I held the earpiece to my left ear and turned the crank on the right.

I have no idea what the voice said, but I panicked. I was sure the police were going to come for me.

I quickly hung up the receiver, climbed down from the chair, put it back at the kitchen table and hid under Mom and Dad's bed. Before long, I heard a noise and crawled out to peek out their bedroom win-dow. It was Mom and Dad, not the police. I never said a word to them, and I never played with that phone again. ❖

Tough Enough

Tough enough for a dogfight, soft enough for a baby's skin." That was the claim of Koroseal by B.F. Goodrich (below) and hundreds of other products developed for American homes.

The space age was not quite upon us in 1949, but the new world of new manmade upholstery, fabrics, containers and luggage was already making life easier—and more durable.

The claims were almost too good to be true: These tough new products could be cleaned easily with soap and water, and "look new and fresh long after other materials would be cut, frayed, stained and old." The material was waterproof, and raincoats, shower curtains and golf jackets "never stick nor crack even if folded away wet." Moths didn't like the new materials, so garment bags and hat boxes kept clothes safer.

OK, maybe the claims overreached more than just a little. But in a world waking up to the wonders of synthetics, "tough enough" was a lot better than what we'd been used to. ❖

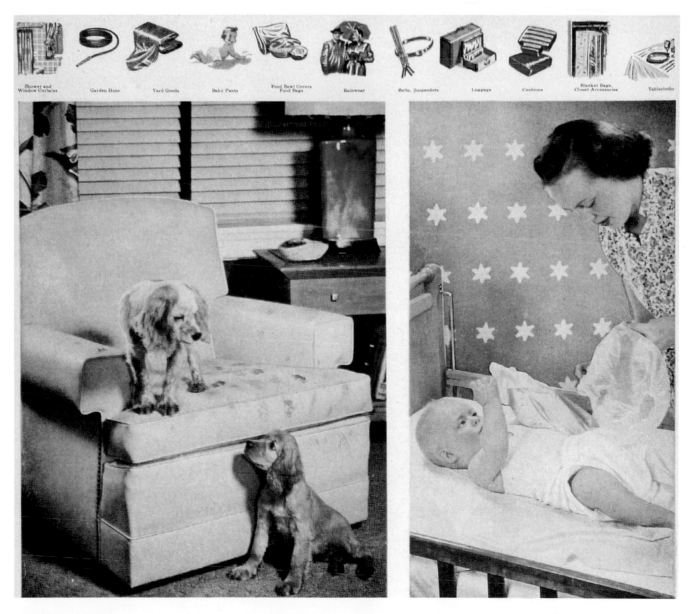

Shower and Window Curtains — Garden Hose — Yard Goods — Baby Pants — Food Bowl Covers, Food Bags — Rainwear — Belts, Suspenders — Luggage — Cushions — Blanket Bags, Closet Accessories — Tablecloths

Warm as Toast

By Janice Barnes

I shiver every time I think of life when I was a youngster before the advent of central heating. Our family lived on a small farm in the mountains of north Arkansas and it wasn't easy to stay warm as toast, that's for sure.

We heated with wood cut from by my father from our own property. Hickory and oak chunks were split and stacked into "ricks"— rows of wood four feet high and eight feet long.

We usually needed 10 to 12 ricks each winter to keep our home warm.

A few years after we married, my husband and I moved lock, stock and barrel to California, where we had our first taste of city life.

One of the biggest changes in our lives was that of how we stayed warm.

No more stacking wood on the porch. No more splitting kindling for starting fires. No more children rushing to the living room from frigid bedrooms in order to dress next to the heating stove. Now we had thermostatically controlled heat.

Honeywell came out with the round thermostat in 1953 and our first "city" home had one. It replaced the chunky, rectangular models from earlier years. I remember the first time we turned the control and heard the furnace roar to life. We had to turn the heat up and down several times to convince ourselves the thermostat indeed would work.

Coming home late from our first evening out, my husband exclaimed something similar to the man in the Timken advertisement (right): "Thank goodness I don't have to fix the furnace!"

Of course, those were the days before central air conditioning joined central heating on the round dial, but you couldn't miss what you had never had.

Sometimes when I think about how we heated our country homes, I wonder how we all stayed as healthy as we did. Memories of those old winter nights back in the Good Old Days are enough to make me all the more thankful today when I relax in my home, warm as toast.

I can tell you that warming up the house simply by turning up the thermostat was *definitely* a whiz-bang wonder to us! ❖

The Crucible of Technology

Honeywell's roll in making the modern world warm as toast dates back to 1885 when an inventor, Albert Butz, patented a furnace regulator and alarm.

Minneapolis Heat Regulator Co. acquired Butz's patents, and MHR merged in 1927 with Honeywell Heating Specialty Co., founded by Mark Honeywell, a young engineer from Wabash, Ind.

Minneapolis-Honeywell, the new name of the merged companies, continued to expand both nationally and internationally during the 1930s and 1940s.

Honeywell's scientific and engineering prowess expanded into aeronautical equipment. In 1942, the company's engineers invented the electronic autopilot, critical to the success of bombing sorties during World War II.

So-o-o Quiet
you can hear your oil bills drop!

Amazing Timken Silent Automatic Wall-Flame Burner guaranteed in writing to cut fuel oil costs up to 25%!

Next time you're in a home with oil heat ...*listen!* If you hear a roaring sound from the furnace, that means *waste!* Wasted fuel oil! Wasted dollars!

Then visit a home that is heated with a Timken Silent Automatic Wall-Flame Burner. What a contrast! There's a tiny click when the motor turns on . . . then *hardly a sound!* That's because of the scientific placement of flame, plus complete preparation of the air-fuel mixture. The result is unequalled, *quietly* efficient operation and *tremendous oil savings!*

These savings over ordinary gun-type oil burners can actually be *guaranteed in writing up to 25%* and frequently amount to far more. And yet they're only one of many *special benefits and savings* offered by Timken Silent Automatic Oil Heat.

Call your local Timken Silent Automatic Dealer. He's listed in the "yellow pages" of your phone book. Ask him about these many advantages . . . and for a free analysis of heating needs. No obligation.

World's Finest, Most Economical Oil Burner

The heart of the Timken Silent Automatic Furnace system is the famous Wall-Flame Burner. It's whisper quiet, clean, and with only one moving part. In addition to its huge fuel savings, it saves *almost two-thirds* in electricity, saves untold dollars in maintenance and repairs. It blankets heating plant walls with a natural, unhurried, blue-hot flame. Gives years and years of trouble-free operation.

The Red-Hot Wonder

By Judith Johnson Matheny

When the truck arrived at our house to deliver a ton of coal every month or so, all the neighborhood kids came to our house, their faces filled with anticipation. The driver opened the hinged metal door and swung the chute from the truck to the opening in the concrete block and into the coal bin.

The din of the coal crashing down the chute and onto the concrete floor of our basement sounded like an avalanche of rock or snow tumbling down a mountainside.

All that coal was destined for the cast-iron monster downstairs.

Modern suburban houses with their high-tech gadgets and creature comforts lack the character of our old house in northwest Detroit, where I grew up. It had a coal-burning furnace! It took up a large portion of the basement, where its round, white, asbestos-wrapped ductwork branched out and upward like tentacles from an octopus. It carried the heat by convection (no electric blowers) through large registers into the rooms of the house.

The furnace door swung open on a hinge (ours always creaked and groaned in protest) and it had a circular vent in the middle to let air in or keep it out, depending on the amount of heat you wanted. There was no thermostat to control the heat as we have on gas, oil and electric furnaces today.

Most of today's young people haven't had the experience of building a fire in a coal furnace, and I feel sad for them.

Furnaces $59⁹⁵ up

It really was an art, and the more you practiced, the more proficient you became.

First you put a few chunks of coal in the firebox, the big hole in the center of the furnace. Then you added a few sticks of wood on top of the coal. The wood had to be dry, or the smoke from it would run you out of the house.

Next, you lit a rolled-up piece of newspaper and used it to ignite the wood, which would eventually light the coal, if you were lucky.

I received a singed finger or two when I held the burning paper too long.

On very cold days, you had to add another shovel of coal and pray you didn't smother the infant flames in the process. The trick was to keep the fire going all day and all night, keeping the house toasty without toasting its inhabitants.

Things that others consider disadvantages of this type of heat didn't seem so to me. The dirt that collected on the walls above the registers was eliminated by frequent paintings. It gave us a good reason to redecorate often. And the ashes that had to be carried out daily were used on icy sidewalks and driveways. We didn't have the expense of buying rock salt, and the ashes served the purpose just as well.

The smell of bituminous coal smoke belching from the chimney might have offended some people, but I liked it. To me, it was a warm, inviting aroma, akin to the smell of a charcoal fire for a summer family barbecue.

Environmentalists might cringe today, but my memories of our coal-burning furnace are warm and happy ones. This relic from the past was truly a red-hot wonder. ❖

It's Cool Inside!

Willis Carrier, the father of air conditioning, was granted a patent for his "apparatus for treating air" in 1906, but it would be nearly 50 years before air conditioners would be used in homes. Until the 1950s, the primary use for air conditioning was industrial and commercial.

After World War II, Americans began to wonder why they couldn't be as cool at home as they were in stores and offices. In 1955, William J. Levitt, one of America's leading homebuilders, predicted that air conditioning would become a basic home feature.

By 1965, 10 percent of American homes were air-conditioned; 30 years later the ratio was up to 75 percent! ❖

My First Typewriter

By Roy Meador

The first of anything treasured in our lives holds special significance, whether it's a first date, first kiss, first love, first automobile or even first typewriter. As a journalist and technical writer, I've owned a substantial number of typewriters—manuals, portables and electronics. Each was important and helped me earn a living. But the old typewriter I remember with greatest fondness was my very first.

My original, beat-up, but tough typewriter didn't get a pet name. I could have named it "Old Blackie" or "The Shadow" or "Wordthrower," but the notion didn't hit me. Yet in the war years of the 1940s, I think it meant even more to me than Old Red, my typewriter today. Sorry about that, Red.

The war was on when I negotiated for my typewriter in the western Oklahoma town of Clinton, slap-dab on Highway 66. I was 15, and I bargained with a fair but sharp dealer who specialized in odds and ends. Some folks called him "Sam the Junkman." Somewhere in his bargain-hunting travels, Sam had acquired a magnificent old Royal manual typewriter.

After some serious haggling, I became the owner of that splendid machine for $15. Frankly, I felt that with that machine, I owned all the possibilities of the world. The financial arrangement was $5 down and $5 on two successive Fridays. I kept faith with both my typewriter and Sam by paying promptly and in full, which may have impressed him since he was famous for telling bill collectors, even on Monday, "Catch me Monday."

Sam insisted that he was letting me have a fabulous bargain. I was old enough and suspicious enough to take that claim with a big grain of salt.

However, when I reflected on the transaction later, I concluded that the odds-and-ends dealer had treated me more generously than I deserved. Guns were higher on the country's priority list than office machines just then, and typewriters for civilians fell within the category of "Wait till the war's over, please." But thanks to Sam, I didn't have to wait. I guess he saw that I was eager to get my hands on the typewriter, and figured he might have trouble finding another buyer. So why not let the kid have it? Whatever the truth, thanks Sam!

Once I owned a typewriter, I faced the next major hurdle: learning to use it with as much skill and speed as the reporters down at the

Clinton newspaper, where I worked part time. Mastering the mechanical operations, such as installing a ribbon, or feeding a sheet of white paper into typing position, was easy enough and fun, too. But I wanted more—much more. I wanted my fingers to dance nimbly over the keys, producing a string of words as if a flash of lightning had dropped from the sky.

Easier said than done.

I knew about touch typing. The newspaper reporters I observed didn't seem to have any standard technique, but they studied their notes as they typed and rarely glanced at the keys. Each had his own strange but efficient two-, three- or four-finger touch system.

I requested and received a lesson in finger placement for touch typing from an old newspaperman called Major. He was speedier on the keyboard than seemed possible as he prepared stories from war reports off the teletype or from the seemingly illegible, chaotic, but thorough notes he took during local interviews.

I didn't know it then, but Major encouraged me to imitate the unique, four-finger typing system he had developed over the years at various small-town newspapers across the Southwest. I soon realized that most self-taught newspaper people typed with odd personal methods that could be amazingly fast, but that also would make typing teachers throw up their hands in shocked protest.

Major's method served him beautifully. But his eccentric system saddled me with bad habits I found hard to break when I eventually borrowed my sister's high-school typing manual.

Then I began painfully mastering the real touch-typing system by applying the oldest and best taskmaster, practice. Thanks anyway, Major, for getting me started on the Royal road

to rapid typing the way those crusty professionals of the press did in the old days.

That Royal manual taught me to type and to write. Using it for countless school papers, letters and stories, I discovered that a typewriter is the best thing ever invented for putting words directly on paper.

In the 1990s, personal computers killed typewriter sales to the point that in 1995, the last major typewriter manufacturer in the United States, Smith Corona, filed for bankruptcy protection. As production went downhill due to computers, we remembered typewriters as the workhorses of offices everywhere and the user-friendliest device for writing ever made.

The Remington Arms Co. began selling the first practical typewriter in 1874. (Mark Twain used one for *The Adventures of Tom Sawyer*.) It was invented by Christopher Latham Sholes and his associates in Milwaukee.

The first Remington was followed by manual, portable and electric models from several manufacturers, including Royal, Underwood and Smith Corona.

For more than a century, typewriters served nationwide as the dominant word-generating machine in offices, schools and homes. Beginning in the 19th century, women proved themselves skilled operators of the remarkable machines. The typewriter made millions of women indispensable employees. My sister Wanda learned to type at about the same time I did and became one of those valued workers, first on a typewriter and later on computers.

The sturdy machines we used back then were amazingly hardy and dependable. I expect my old $15 Royal can still turn out a good-looking page. For hard work and duties done but not forgotten, thanks, Royal pal. ❖

Wall-to-Wall Comfort

"Newfangled" was bestowed upon so many of the whiz-bang wonders of the 20th century.

Cars, appliances, electric razors and so many other innovations—all seemed to be called "newfangled" at one time or another.

But floor covering? Could that be new-fangled, too? Well, in 1933 at the Century of Progress Exposition in Chicago, a new type of floor covering was introduced to challenge the old standby of linoleum. It was vinyl, and it made a big splash in that not-so-flashy world.

But the introduction was rather ill-timed. World War II brought a scarcity of vinyl, so vinyl flooring was not widely marketed until the late 1940s.

Then the rush was on—much like a Baby Boom child into the outstretched arms of her father. At first it was used only for

high-traffic areas. However, as demand grew, vinyl became the flooring of choice for almost any place that wasn't covered by carpet.

The demand was even higher when the 1960s brought cushioned and "no-wax" floors.

The newfangled world of vinyl was—and is—second only to carpeting for covering our floors back in the whiz-bang era.

In some regards, not much had changed in carpet production in a long, long time.

A case in point: Mohawk Carpet Mills began in 1878 in Amsterdam, N.Y., with 14 secondhand looms shipped from England.

Carpet weaving and texture remained essentially the same until the company introduced the first sculptured carpet in the late 1930s.

The company built new weaving facilities in Mississippi and South Carolina in the 1950s.

In 1956, Mohawk and Alexander Smith Inc. merged to form Mohasco Industries, at that time the largest carpet manufacturer in the world.

But what the expansion meant for most of us was that carpets became cheaper and readily available for American homeowners.

Nothing was warmer on little feet than carpet and woven rugs. And never in the history of the United States had so many little feet been pitter-pattering.

From the Century of Progress to the Baby Boom, our living rooms were covered with wall-to-wall comfort. ❖

Tommy Mohawk

The Tommy Mohawk character was created for Mohawk Carpet by the Walt Disney Studios in 1951. Tommy Mohawk starred in a series of animated television commercials, and appeared in countless print advertisements as well.

The character went on to become one of the most recognizable and effective company mascots in the history of American business.

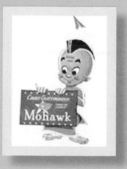

Mealtime Miracles

Chapter Two

*I*t seemed like home life revolved around the kitchen and mealtime miracles were happening by the droves back in the whiz-bang years. In every corner of the kitchen, chores were becoming easier, faster, tastier and—some would argue—healthier.

Just think of the change brought about by the refrigerator! In the 1930s and even into the 1940s, most folks in towns and cities relied on the icebox and the venerable iceman to keep food from spoiling. On the farm, it was likely to be a springhouse that cooled milk and other perishables. Breads and some baked desserts could fill the kitchen with their aroma, but generally mothers prepared Monday's meals on Monday.

With the refrigerator came a taste of freedom. Food could be kept longer; snacks and even entire meals could be prepared and then stored

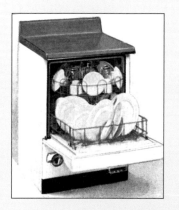

for refrigerator raids, whether by youngsters after school, families at the supper table or husbands late at night.

The cousin of the refrigerator was the freezer. Now meat could be frozen rather than canned, smoked or cured. Moms and wives could package fruits and vegetables and toss them into the freezer instead of spending hot, sweaty hours over a steaming canner. In the old days—unless your home was blessed with an outdoor, open-air summer kitchen—summer days were even steamier thanks to all the winter food preparation.

Freedom was a byproduct of all of the miracles happening in the kitchen. Janice, my dear wife, spent much less time in the kitchen than her mother did. Stoves and ovens were much more reliable and efficient (even if they weren't as quick as today's microwaves). It was easier to wrap up leftovers for a snack. Dishwashers helped homemakers breeze through the cleanup. And that is to say nothing about that wonderful innovation called the TV dinner—how did we get along without that?

Yes, mealtime miracles meant a lot to mothers and wives back in the Good Old Days.

—Ken Tate

Country Kitchen

By Helen Colwell Oakley

The day electricity finally came to our New York state farmhouse in the 1930s set off a whirlwind of changes. Our country kitchen had been an old-fashioned one, but not anymore, for Mom ordered a brand-new Hotpoint electric range! I can still remember how beautiful it was, all sparkling white, trimmed with touches of shiny chrome.

Everyone thought Mom would toss out the old, black, wood-burning heating and cooking stove now that she had an electric one. But for some reason, the woodstove remained through the years, along with Mom's pride and joy, her new electric cooking range.

Mom was justifiably proud of the new range, for it was the only one for miles around that had a fancy deep-well cooker. How magical it seemed to have stew, soup or a pot roast steaming away, completely out of sight except for the cover on the stove's surface.

Dad humored Mom about her adoration of the new stove (it was known as "the new stove" for many years). In fact, I must admit that we *all* forgot about the many wonders of our old, black heating stove

that summer—until fall's chilly mornings and evenings suddenly arrived. It didn't do any good to huddle close to the new stove; it didn't give out much heat, not like the old woodstove, anyway.

One morning, Dad started a fire in Old Faithful. Then it was heavenly in our cozy country kitchen, with the teakettle singing and coffee percolating enticingly for breakfast. Mom soon blacked up the top of the old stove and we all decided that it didn't look so bad after all, especially when we realized how much a part of us it really was—keeping us cozy and warm, and cooking and baking country fare to perfection.

After sitting unnoticed for several months while we basked in the wonders of

Mom's new range, the old cooking stove was in the limelight once again. How wonderful it was to have extra water warming in the reservoir, and the teakettle always hot for emergencies.

It was wonderful to not worry about things boiling or simmering over and have Mom fussing about messes on her nice, new electric range. When we cooked pancakes, sausages and eggs on the electric range, it was a sorry sight. But when we used the old griddle on the old stove, no one cared how messy it was.

When the holidays rolled around, we wondered how we could have survived without the old woodstove. Mom used it to roast the hams, turkeys and chickens, and bake the large Hubbard squashes. She simmered brown-sugar beans on it all day and kept the stovetop covered with a variety of kettles bubbling with vegetables and sauces. Overhead, a clothes rack lined with clothing aired and dried most every day.

The old stove was perfect in every way, except when the chimney burned out. How terrifying it was, rumbling and roaring, and sending sparks and flames out onto the rooftop!

After that scare, we were careful to have the chimney cleaned more often.

Much as we dreaded chimney fires, we were soon drawn back to the warmth and convenience of the old wood range. And so it remained in the country kitchen down through the years. Our old stove baked the best cookies and pies, all tinged with brown and tasty as could be, flavored with Mom's pork lard. The baked hams, roast turkeys and chickens that came out of that old stove were truly delicious.

We didn't forget Mom's new stove. It was delightful to cook in the hot summertime without heating the kitchen up, like the old stove did. And Mom enjoyed cooking on her new stove, especially with the deep-well cooker.

The new electric range lasted for more than 50 years, standing side by side with the old cookstove. Mom only seemed to have it repaired after severe thunderstorms; lightning burned out the wiring several times. Folks often talked about the number of years Mom used her new electric range. Her combination of the old and the new worked for us. ❖

The Icebox Versus The Frigidaire

By Paula Van Cleave

In 1936, we lived in a four-family upper flat on LaBelle Avenue in Highland Park, Mich. That year, my father, a World War I veteran, was hospitalized with tuberculosis. My mom had an eighth-grade education.

She did housework—scrubbing floors, cleaning windows, doing laundry—to support my brother, 10, and me, 9. Her hard work paid the $15-a-month rent and put food on the table.

My brother had a paper route. I helped him, selling papers on a corner at night while he took his papers to the restaurants. I also baby-sat and took four kindergartners to school.

Every little bit we earned contributed to our family's survival.

We had what we called a window box on the outside windowsill, and in the winter, we stored our perishable food there to keep it cold. In the summer we used an icebox in the kitchen. Under the icebox was a pan that caught the water that dripped off the melting ice. My brother was assigned the task of emptying the drip pan on odd days, and I had to do it on even days. The pan filled every 8–10 hours. Needless to say, the flat below us had a leaky ceiling from our own negligence and that of former tenants.

The ice was brought regularly by the iceman, who drove through the neighborhood delivering ice from the back of his truck. Do you remember the old ice truck? We used to grab small pieces of ice from it and catch a ride on the back.

Mom worked for a wonderful woman, Mrs. Spreen. When she appropriated a new refrigerator, she offered her old one to Mom. Mrs. Spreen just needed a larger box; for us, though, a refrigerator meant getting rid of the icebox *and* that aggravating drip pan.

When Mom told us about the refrigerator, we couldn't wait. Some weeks passed, but finally, one day, Mrs. Spreen hired a truck and our refrigerator was delivered.

That refrigerator was the weirdest-looking thing. It had a large, round apparatus on top—apparently it had something to do with the cooling—*and* no drip pan.

We were the only people with a refrigerator for blocks around, and we were the talk of the neighborhood. My brother and I took advantage of the opportunity by charging people three cents to come in and see it. If they wanted to look inside, it cost two cents more! We had a steady stream of people coming through our house, including folks from many streets away—people we never heard from or saw again. If my mom had known what we were doing, she'd have strapped us—especially me, because she always called me the instigator of all troubles.

No longer did we have to put the "ICE" sign in our window for the iceman. Also ended were our hassles with that darned drip pan, which caused so much conflict in our young lives.

But the really big loser in this drama was the corner penny candy store. With all the pennies we collected showing off our newfangled refrigerator that summer, I would venture to guess it lost a fortune. ❖

With great affection, I said:
"I am going to write to General Electric--"

This 17-year-old G-E Refrigerator is the model described by Mrs. Miller in glowing terms.

Few writers have ever expressed so sincere a feeling about a product as did Mrs. May G. Miller, of Bellflower, Calif., in this letter to us. She wrote:

"I was cleaning my refrigerator this morning, and as I looked at it with great affection, I said: 'Do you know what I am going to do? I am going to write to General Electric and tell them about you. Big people like to hear nice things as well as little people.'

"My G-E Refrigerator has been in constant use for going on seventeen years. It has never been idle one day, and has never had one thing wrong with it. It has in all that time just given service, service, service. Do you wonder that I feel about it as I do?"

Service—today's yardstick of refrigerators

Nothing could please us more than to know that our G-E Refrigerators have won the abiding loyalty of users like Mrs. Miller.

For today we aren't making new refrigerators. And we know that those we *have* made must keep going . . . to give the efficient home refrigeration that's so necessary in preserving wartime food.

This means that the single yardstick of refrigerator value today is *service*—care-free, trouble-free service. And we're very glad that G-E Refrigerators are measuring up exceptionally well.

TUNE IN: "The G-E All-Girl Orchestra," Sunday, 10 p. m., E. W. T., NBC—"The World Today" news, every weekday, 6:45 p. m., E. W. T., CBS.

Wartime Reminder: Your General Electric Dealer is as anxious as we are to see that *every* G-E Refrigerator keeps giving efficient home refrigeration. He's doing a great job . . . but because of the manpower shortage, he's under a serious handicap. So it's up to you to give your refrigerator the best of care at all times. General Electric Company, Bridgeport, Conn.

BUY AND HOLD WAR BONDS! KEEP ON BUYING THEM!

Here is the latest model G-E Refrigerator, shown in the all-electric kitchen you'll soon be able to have.

GE Refrigerators

A MILLION IN SERVICE TEN YEARS OR LONGER

GENERAL *GE* ELECTRIC

A Cool History

The modern history of refrigeration goes back to the early 19th century and Michael Faraday, an Englishman who experimented with using liquefied ammonia to create a cooling effect. Faraday's work progressed through many modifications in the next century until the first home refrigerator was introduced by General Electric in Fort Wayne, Ind., in 1911. Fort Wayne was also home to the first Frigidaire—under the name of "Guardian"—four years later.

The market proliferated and by 1920, more than 200 models were available.

To say that early refrigerators were impractical for the average home is an understatement. The compressor was belt-driven by a motor that was usually in an adjoining room or even in the basement. What we would consider the first modern models were not produced until after World War II.

The first freezers were introduced in the 1920s and '30s, but it would be the 1940s before frozen-food storage was commonly used.

Defrosting the freezer compartment prompted probably the single biggest complaint about the refrigerator. We thought we had left the drip pan behind with the departure of the icebox, but defrosting meant mopping the kitchen floor, unless you had one of the models with a pan underneath.

The late 1950s brought automatic-defrost models, and they proliferated during the 1960s. This innovation meant no more freezer compartments filled almost entirely with accumulated frost.

The years of refrigeration are filled with a cool history that made mealtime miracles possible. ❖

Look Mom... NO HANDS!

QUICKFREEZER

Before you buy, see the

VICTOR QUICKFREEZER with the New Pedal-Dor!

Hazardous to Your Health

It may be true that the use of freon beginning in the 1930s may have endangered the Earth's ozone layer, but refrigerators posed a danger to consumers much earlier than that!

Refrigerators from the late 1800s until 1929 used the toxic gases ammonia, methylene chloride and sulfur dioxide as refrigerants.

Several fatal accidents occurred in the 1920s when methylene chloride leaked out of refrigerators.

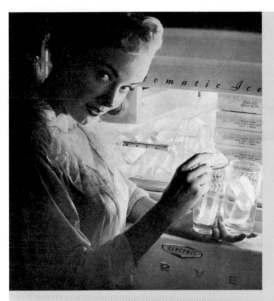

Tray Bonne!

Today we take for granted the ice-cube trays included in the freezers of most modern refrigerators. Did you know that the modern ice-cube tray may have gotten its start in the medical field?

In 1844, Dr. John Goorie was concerned about the high temperatures of his yellow-fever patients. He built a refrigerator to make ice to cool the air in his clinic. Some authorities say he also may have invented the first ice-cube tray.

The first flexible tray was invented in 1933 by Guy Tinkham, vice president of the General Utilities Co. The tray cost 50 cents.

Keeping It Cool

Today we hardly give ice a second thought. If we need ice for a drink or to pack a picnic ice chest, we simply go to the freezer or pick up a bag at the store. Keeping it cool in the Good Old Days was a much tougher prospect.

The chore began in the winter, when men with teams of horses scored the ice on a thickly frozen lake (bottom photo). Then ice blocks were sawed (below left) and taken to the community icehouse for storage (below right).

The invention of the freezer made it so much easier to have a bucket of ice on hand for entertaining. It's hard to believe, but the ice industry celebrated a century of "ice progress" in the whiz-bang year of 1950. ❖

Did You Know?

The ice trade between Boston and the South was one of the first casualties of the Civil War.

What Three-letter Word Chills Beverages Without Killing the Taste?

If you've ever been served a beverage filled with cloudy, fast-melting ice cubes and tasting faintly of yesterday's broccoli, you know why really smart hosts and hostesses use nothing but *genuine* ice.

For *genuine* ice—the kind made *only* by your Ice Company—is not only hard-frozen and crystal-clear but as completely *taste-free* as the purest water. It is inexpensive to buy—convenient and wonderful to use.

The next time you plan a party, be sure to have plenty of *genuine* ice on hand to ensure its success. Your Ice Company will gladly supply your needs.

NATIONAL ASSOCIATION OF ICE INDUSTRIES
Dept. SA, 1706 L Street, N.W., Washington 6, D. C.

Genuine ICE FILLS EVERY COOLING NEED

When You Entertain
Use crushed ice generously in serving appetizers, juices, sea-foods and salads. Your Ice Company can supply *genuine* ice for every occasion.

When You Shop
Get your money's worth when you buy vegetables! Up-to-date stores always keep their vegetables *garden-fresh* by displaying them in *crushed ice.*

Home-Made Ice Cream
Old-fashioned, velvety ice cream made with *genuine* ice in a home freezer has a texture and flavor no "still-frozen" substitute can equal.

Free Money-Saver
Send a postcard today for your *free* copy of "Money-saving Tips on Marketing"— a complete guide to buying vegetables, poultry, sea-food.

Ice Makes The Picnic
Picnic time calls for *genuine* ice and plenty of it. A handy picnic chest carries the ice— and the beverages—and keeps the foods fresh besides. Inexpensive, too. Get one from your local Ice Company.

1850—ONE HUNDRED YEARS OF ICE PROGRESS—1950

Wrapping It Up!

By Kay Blevins

Wow! Did our lives ever change as we discovered more and more ways to wrap and store our food, whether it came from our gardens or from our local grocer!

A good example of how packaging changed our lives is the delivery of milk. Remember the milkman and the heavy returnable glass bottles of old? I know I do. That began to change in 1915 when Pure-Pak cartons were patented.

It was the early 1930s before industrial

SMART WAY TO BUY—
Cheese in **Pliofilm** is never dry or crumbly.

Handiest Food Saver You Ever Used!
Save money by keeping foods and leftovers many extra days in **Pliofilm**—sold in 12- and 18-inch rolls. Can be washed and used over and over again.

Pliofilm

machines were developed and the cartons could go into mass production, but the wax-coated cartons were making milk bottles a thing of the past by the late 1940s and early 1950s, even in cities—the last bastion of the milkman.

Up until the 1950s, Pure-Pak cartons had a pull-tab on the side of the gable (note arrow pointing to tab location on the Pure-Pak ad on the facing page). The familiar spout of today was a whiz-bang wonder of the mid-1950s.

Products like Pliofilm and DuPont's Cellophane made wrapping, refrigeration and freezing safer and so much more convenient. You could actually see what was wrapped in the package, whether at the market or in the refrigerator.

Then there is the ubiquitous twist tie. Today it is used on just about every kind of plastic bag, from bread to garbage.

T and T Industries is credited with inventing the twist tie, and its Twist-Ems brand of ties was the first to be issued a U.S. patent. Founded in 1942, the company is still in business today as one of the largest manufacturers of ties in the United States.

By the early 1960s, there were many makers of twist ties, including Plas-Ties Corp., which touted its product with the claim: "Twist … it's open! Twist … it's closed!" Some consumers trying to untwist a twist tie might dispute that claim, but the little paper- or plastic-covered wire continues to be one of the most ingenius products of the whiz-bang years.

I remember my first Tupperware party—don't you? They were an innovation in themselves, a

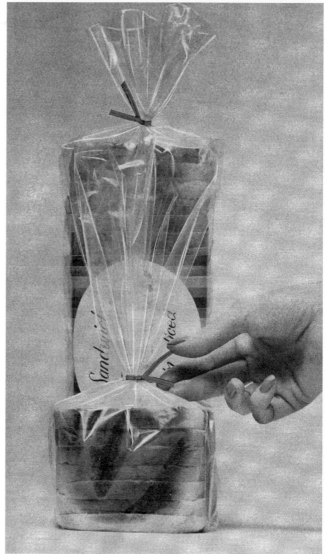

TWIST…IT'S OPEN!
TWIST…IT'S CLOSED!

way for the manufacturer to bring the little containers directly to homemakers like you and me.

The idea began with the invention of the seal by Earl Silas Tupper in 1947. His polyethylene containers and airtight lids kept foods fresher longer in the refrigerator.

But Tupper and his fledgling company had problems marketing the containers through retail stores, mainly because consumers couldn't figure out how to use the lids and because retail salesmen didn't know how to demonstrate.

By 1951, Tupper had pulled all Tupperware products out of stores and began the parties that almost all homemakers of the 1950s and '60s attended. Today the company estimates that a demonstration party begins every two seconds somewhere in the world, and annual net sales total in excess of $1 billion.

I don't know about you, but the little container that could was sure a mealtime miracle for me!

But it may have been the innovation of the individually wrapped serving that most clearly reflected the trend toward individualism that marked the whiz-bang years.

Now drinks, chips, desserts and breakfast cereal all were offered individually packaged.

I remember when Post Cereal came out with its Post-Ten package of individual packages of the company's most popular brands. Our children sure enjoyed picking from the 10 small boxes for their breakfast!

Of course, the coolest thing about this was that you didn't even need a bowl. There were instructions that showed how to open the box along the back-panel perforations, carefully slit open the inner wrap and pour the milk right in. Then you could eat it right from the box!

Yes, I'll never forget how all of that changed our lives back in the Good Old Days. ❖

The choosiest people
just happen to choose Post-Tens

Pick your own breakfast.
Eight great cereals (even new Post Alpha-Bits)
in ten individual boxes . . . a different one for
every member of the family. And every one
loaded with fun, flavor and plenty of nutrition.

All Post cereals happen to be just a little bit better!

TV Dinners: Meals on the Go

What more epitomized the whiz-bang era than the development of the frozen TV dinner by Swanson Foods in 1952? It had all the elements important to the popular culture of the day: It was convenient, it was tasty and, at least in name, it involved the television.

TV dinners were a boon to working women who had remained on the job after World War II.

The concept signaled the rapid expansion of fast-food restaurants (the first franchised McDonald's opened in 1955) and convenience food.

The TV dinner was developed because Swanson had too many turkeys. Most turkey meat was sold around Thanksgiving in those days, and the company had nothing else to do with the meat but keep it in cold storage.

Gerry Thomas, one of Swanson Food's

product developers, envisioned a solution to the problem: a single-serving, complete turkey dinner in one frozen package.

The original TV dinner contained sliced turkey, cornbread dressing, gravy, sweet potatoes and buttered peas.

The food was processed in such a way that when the consumer cooked it, each of the foods was hot and ready to eat at the same time.

The dinner was frozen in a three-compartment aluminum tray.

Thomas said later that he came up with the name "TV dinner" because of the exploding popularity of the new medium. The aluminum tray was even designed to resemble the front of a television.

Little did the company know that many Americans would assume that TV dinners were to be eaten in front of the TV—and thus was engendered another cultural phenomenon. ❖

Quick, Fast & In a Hurry

*M*eals on the go didn't begin and end with TV dinners. It seemed that the entire culture was headed toward food that could be prepared in a snap. In other words—like the old saying—we wanted meals that could be on the table "quick, fast and in a hurry." The food industry was doing all it could to keep up with demand.

Case in point: Tang. General Foods scientist William Mitchell (who died July 26, 2004) came up with a formula for a new orange-flavored, instant, powdered breakfast drink in the mid-1950s. But for almost a decade, the product languished, even though it had been available as early as 1959.

Then came an agreement with NASA, and Tang became "the drink of the astronauts." The drink was carried on every manned space flight from 1965 to 1972. It was a marketer's dream! General Foods began a new ad campaign and the drink soared in popularity.

Moms were thrilled that their children were getting the recommended amount of vitamin C. Kids were even more thrilled that they were drinking the same thing the astronauts did. With every space mission, sales went up like a rocket!

"Miracles" seemed to be the catchword, even apart from the space race and Tang.

Minute Maid (originally the National Research Corp.) first developed a way to concentrate orange juice in powder form and used the product to keep troops healthy during World War II.

Then, in the late 1940s, the company discovered a way to freeze the liquefied juice concentrate and—*voila!*—we could have orange juice for breakfast year round.

Speaking of breakfast and miracles, the choice adult beverage for breakfast has long been coffee. A "new miracle way to cream your coffee"— Pream—hit the market in the mid-1950s.

A Real Chef!

Unlike Betty Crocker and Aunt Jemima, one culinary icon was not, as commonly believed, a fictional person. Chef Boyardee was born Hector Boiardi in northern Italy in 1898.

Hector worked in restaurant kitchens from the age of 11 before immigrating to America at age 17. After working at renowned hotel kitchens in New York and West Virginia, he opened his own restaurant, *Il Giardino d'Italia*, in Cleveland, Ohio.

Boiardi's spaghetti sauce soon became famous throughout Cleveland, and patrons began asking him for extra portions. He obliged, giving them milk bottles filled with the sauce.

Demand for his spaghetti sauce grew, and he started producing it in an adjacent loft. He sold it with dry pasta and packets of his special cheese.

Chef Boiardi changed the spelling of his name to an Americanized "Boyardee," and moved his operations to Pennsylvania before eventually merging with American Home Foods and now ConAgra Foods.

He continued to work with the brand that bore his name until his death in 1985.

Breakfast wasn't the only meal of the day, however; we were also looking for quick, but nutritious ways to prepare dinner and supper. Scientists were promising a push-button world, and we wanted push-button meals to go with it.

That's what Van Camp's promised in the summer of 1948. Actually, Frank Van Camp began marketing his canned baked beans (above) in the late 19th century, and the label had become the favorite pork-and-bean product by the early 1900s. Like any good company, Van Camp's was constantly reinventing itself, and the "quick foods" market offered a perfect avenue for repositioning this mature product.

How many other quick meals can you think of? Certainly the Chef Boyardee products come to mind (see sidebar, right). The spaghetti and meatballs were great, but who can forget a name like Beefaroni? Whenever a mother needed a quick meal, the Chef was always there.

Some meals just made you feel better. Mama's chicken noodle soup was the prescription for anyone with a cold—or anyone without one, for that matter. But what happened when Mama was too busy to whip up a pot of it? Campbell's soup came to the rescue!

One Campbell's ad (see facing page) from the mid-1950s even noted the extensive directions for making a pot of chicken noodle soup like theirs. Later, in the 1960s, "soup and sandwich" became the Campbell's mantra for a quick and nutritious lunch.

But the main course wasn't all that was on the minds of kids and their parents. The sweet tooth was aching for something quick, fast and in a hurry as well.

We certainly didn't have to crank out ice cream any longer. Buckets, cartons and individual servings were all available at our friendly neighborhood grocery store.

Then there were quick cinnamon rolls from Pillsbury, showing us that biscuits weren't the only thing that could come from a can.

And if Minute Rice from Uncle Ben was available, could Minute Tapioca be far behind?

Quick, fast and in a hurry—that is how mealtime miracles were made back in the Good Old Days. ❖

How to make chicken noodle soup like *Campbell's*

Well, first of all, you do it the patient, old-fashioned way. The way your great grandma did, back in the days when a woman practically *lived* in the kitchen. For making this delicious soup is a fussy and time-taking job. Chicken simmered slowly to make that good flavorful broth. Then all the breast and leg meat carefully taken from the bones and diced. And, of course, the *noodles!*

Egg noodles rolled out with a light hand to keep them tender. But *today*, why should you go to all this bother! You can get Campbell's Chicken Noodle Soup anywhere. Rich broth that glistens with chicken goodness. Plenty of tempting pieces of chicken. And lots of golden noodles.

Yours to enjoy—within 3 or 4 minutes after opening the can.

Cooking With Gas

By Pat Fitzmaurice

Back when I was a youngster in the hills of southern Missouri, we burned wood both for heating and for cooking. I remember, in the 1940s, when we were able to finally modernize and for the first time had gas for cooking (gas heat would come a few years later).

"Now you're cooking with gas!" was a popular phrase, meaning that you were up-to-date—"with it," as some would say in later years.

Cooking with gas meant that Mama could have even heat when preparing our meals. The old wood cookstove wasn't always the most accurate, which meant Mama and all other old-time cooks did more baking by instinct than by recipe.

Getting a gas stove also meant that our home wasn't nearly as hot during summer months. Our new, whiz-bang stove had an oven the was actually insulated! The four gas burners no longer sat atop a roaring firebox. Once a dish was cooked, the burner or oven was turned off. You didn't have to wait for the fire to die out before the room started to cool down.

How Mama loved cooking with gas! We always had a huge garden and she canned hundreds

Entertaining or every-day, GAS makes cooking fast, cool and clean on this fabulous new TAPPAN

TAPPAN

CONTROLLED — WITH GAS. Burner-with-a Brain* guards your Hollandaise sauce! Controls cooking temperature so even delicate foods won't scorch, burn, or boil over. Regulates itself automatically.

FLAME-BROWNED — WITH GAS. Even Crème Brulée is a triumph. Easy: with fast Gas broiling; sure: with Tappan's accurate controls. And shut-door Gas broiling keeps you and your kitchen delightfully cool.

SAFE — WITH GAS. Oven, broiler, all burners light automatically, all over. If oven or broiler pilot goes out, this tiny "sentry" device shuts off the Gas automatically.

Help like this makes parties fun! Try new recipes you never dared before—make old favorites newly great—with automatic controls to smooth every step. Have perfect roasts—with even Gas heat, *automatic* meat thermometer. Enjoy succulent barbecues—flame-browned, basted *automatically*. Sauces you never knew *you* could do are safe *automatically*, on the Burner-with-a-Brain. Guests late? No panic—"Keep-Warm" oven control (140°) holds meals "table ready" for hours *without overcooking*. This new, fabulously-styled Tappan "400" is a superb example of ranges built to Gold Star standards. At your Gas company or appliance dealer's.   AMERICAN GAS ASSOCIATION

Easy modernizer: build this TAPPAN in, hang on a wall, or slide it in!

LIVE MODERN FOR LESS WITH **GAS**

WHEN YOU SEE THIS GOLD STAR ON A RANGE, YOU KNOW IT COOKS FASTER, COOLER, CLEANER — AUTOMATICALLY!

*A.G.A. Mark ©Am. Gas Assoc., Inc.

of quarts of green beans, peas, tomatoes and beets each year.

Her canning was much more efficient and our house wasn't nearly as hot as a result. Summer nights were sweltering enough without waiting for the cookstove to cool down.

Years later, kitchens were modernized again. By that time I was married, with my own children. The all-electric kitchen was the rage at that time, and my wife and I decided to give it a try, even though I was rather dubious.

If anything, our new electric cookstove was even more efficient and cooler to cook on than our old gas stove. Today the microwave oven has them all beat.

But when I think about the huge difference it made when we finally added our first modern stove, I know I have a much deeper appreciation for the marvels of the whiz-bang world.

Besides, "cooking with electricity" just doesn't have the ring of "Now you're cooking with gas!" ❖

Cooking Without Gas

By Bernard R. DeRemer

We cooked and heated the kitchen with a stove just like the one pictured below when we lived in St. Paris, Ohio, during the booming 1920s and busted '30s.

Our home was typical; hot water and automatic central heating existed only for the favored few, not *hoi polloi* like us.

But from this stove my aunt and foster mother served up delicious meals thrice daily, and baked on special occasions.

The black monster devoured tons of soft coal, which I shoveled into a bucket and lugged into the kitchen from the coal bin adjacent to the old summer kitchen. At least I didn't have to go outdoors, braving rain, snow or wind for those trips—but it was almost as cold as it was outside.

Satisfying its appetite for fuel was, of course, only part of the routine. Ashes had to be cleaned out, carried to the edge of the alley and dumped. I handled these chores before and after school (when I couldn't get out of them). In fact, I did the same things for a couple of neighbors, picking up a few coins for Saturday-night spending sprees at the Gen Theater and Clark's Drug Store.

The stove boasted a reservoir that was filled with rainwater for washing ourselves and our dishes. I understand that it yielded better results than hard water, and saved soap as well. (Whatever happened to cisterns, anyway?) The best you could say about it was that the contents were warm rather than cold, and there was no waiting.

A base burner heated the large living room (actually a double room) when fed sufficient quantities of hard coal or coke.

It boasted isinglass windows over the front and sides; what a welcome, cheery sight that bright blaze presented when we got within view of it, trudging home from downtown on cold winter nights! It was ideal for toasting marshmallows, too.

The upstairs was another world, totally devoid of heat. I hated that frigid bedroom; how wonderful an electric blanket would have been!

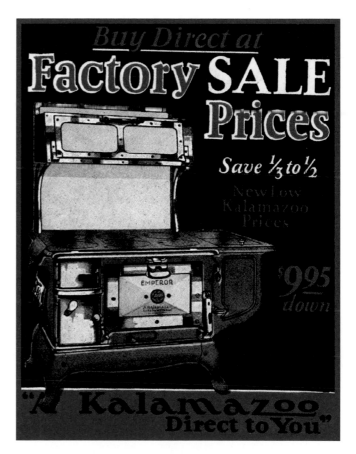

In the years since, I have sometimes found myself in a city apartment where the heat simply couldn't be turned off. You could turn the radiator valve until doomsday; it accomplished precisely nothing. I think I despised that even more! Why do we so often have to go from one extreme to the other?

Let us now praise the wonders of automatic heat and individual room thermostats, microwave ovens and other modern marvels—then trickle a tear or two for all those hardy pioneers "born 30 or more years too soon." ❖

Stirring Things Up

Nothing had a way of stirring things up in the kitchen like small appliances did. Anyone who knows what it meant to make whipped cream with a spoon or a hand-beater knows how wonderful it was the first time she whipped it up with a mixer. Mixers, blenders, grinders and all of their appliance cousins made life in the kitchen all the more convenient back in the Good Old Days.

There were many different types of mixers dating all the way back to the late 1800s, but the first truly consumer mixer was the Mixmaster made by Sunbeam in 1930. Sunbeam products were mainstays in the American kitchen, from coffee percolators to toasters.

The blender was another wonder that stirred things up. The first blender was invented in 1922 by Stephen Poplawski and was used primarily to blend soda fountain drinks.

Fred Waring (yes, the big band man that fronted Fred Waring and the Pennsylvanians) bankrolled several innovations to the Poplawski design and finally the Waring Blender was born.

It's hard to say if Waring was better-known for the music or the blender.

The Osterizer was another brand that improved on the Poplawski design. John Oster had founded his company in 1922, specializing in barber tools. In 1946, Oster purchased Stevens Electric Co., which specialized in home appliances.

The Osterizer made blending and chopping vegetables a snap, but the Oster engineers weren't done. In 1955, the company came out with a two-speed version of its blender. Could 12-speed models be far behind?

So, what appliance stirred things up in the kitchen the most? Maybe one you wouldn't think about.

In 1927, inventor John Hammes built his wife what is regarded as the world's first garbage disposal unit. After 10 years of improving on his original design, Hammes began marketing his appliance, the "In-Sink-Erator"—to the public. By the late 1950s, in-sink garbage disposals were a household staple.

Whew! Talk about stirring things up! ❖

Dishwashing Days

By Donna McGuire Tanner

Dishes, dishes everywhere. On the kitchen and dining room tables, on the cabinets, there were stacks of dirty dishes, pots and pans everywhere. As far back as I can remember, it was always my job to do the dishes for our very large family at our home in Pax, W.Va.

It was a long, boring, lonely job. I spent so much time in the kitchen with my hands in the dishpan full of water that whenever I signed my name, I actually added "M.D." (McGuire Dishwasher).

It was a happy day for me but a sad one for my sister, Brenda, when our parents, Basil and Rachel, decided she was finally old enough to dry the dishes. What a glorious day that was! I had help at last.

Our house had an open invitation to everyone: friends, neighbors and

kin. So there were always never-ending dishes. Brenda and I would keep water heating on the coal stove at all times for refilling the dishpans.

To pass the time, we watched the neighborhood activity through the kitchen window as we worked. In winter, we saw children sledding down the steep road in front of our house. In the summer, there were more people going up and down the road to gossip about. "Must be Wednesday, they are dressed for prayer meeting," we'd say as we watched the elderly couple go down the road in their car.

My sister and I found other ways to break the boredom. We brought the radio into the kitchen and danced the latest steps while we worked. The faster the music, the more quickly we finished the job.

Sometimes we sang to the music, or if the radio wasn't playing, we made up our own words to familiar songs, such as, "I've been washing dishes all the livelong day!" Our last name was McGuire, but the famous McGuire Sisters we weren't.

One evening we were singing at the top of our lungs. I was just finishing the last line of *Take Me Out to the Ballgame* as I went to fetch another stack of plates from the dining room table.

I heard muffled laughter coming from the living room, which faced the dining room. I turned to see that my older brother, Danny, had brought home some of his friends, including some of our classmates. The room was filled, and Brenda and I were the unsuspecting entertainment.

I pivoted and ran into the kitchen, minus dishes. When Brenda saw my beet-red face, she asked what was wrong. I could only manage to motion toward the other room.

Brenda wiped her hands on her apron and went to investigate. A few seconds later, she was back in the kitchen, her hands covering her crimson face. As we listened to the laughter echoing through the house, she said what I was thinking: "I'm going to die! I'm *never* going back to school again!"

Then we both said, "Let's get him!"—meaning Danny. Of course, our parents saved our brother from two angry sisters, and we did go to school, and we did live through the embarrassment to tell our children about our dishwashing days. ❖

Automatic Dishwashers

Most of us did our fair share of dishwashing back in the Good Old Days. And then came the era of the automatic dishwasher.

But the first practical automatic dishwasher was invented in 1886 in Shelbyville, Ill., by Josephine Cochrane. She was a rich woman who entertained often, and she had servants to wash her dishes. But she wanted a device that would do the job faster and not break as many dishes.

Did she hire someone to design a dishwasher for her? No, she designed and built it herself!

She unveiled her new machine at the 1893 Chicago World's Fair, and won the show's highest award.

Interest grew quickly, especially from restaurants and hotels in Illinois, so Mrs. Cochrane patented the design and went into production. Her company grew into what is now the well-known KitchenAid Corp.

As for using automatic dishwashers in the average household—well, that was altogether another story.

The machines were too big and expensive for regular homes. They were powered by steam, and dishes moved on a conveyor belt as they were sprayed by jets of hot water.

It wasn't until the whiz-bang years of the 1950s, when automatic dishwashers finally became cheaper and smaller, that homeowners finally bought into the concept of an automatic dishwasher—besides the kids!

Mother's Little Helpers

Chapter Three

I am amazed when I think of how the world has changed since I was a little boy. I can remember watching my grandmother sweep her floors with a handmade broom of straw. Grandma also used sadirons and a treadle Singer sewing machine. Both my mother and Janice's washed clothes on scrub boards with lye soap before electricity came to the farm.

Then came all those homemaker helpers of the whiz-bang era.

The first big innovation for my childhood home was the venerable wringer washer. I remember to this day getting fingers pulled into the wringer as I helped Mama soon after we got the machine. I was feeding clothes from the rinse tub and didn't realize the force with which the rollers pulled the laundry. Later on, an automatic release was added that separated and disengaged the rollers if fingers or too-thick clothes (like overalls) got stuck. But our first machine was not so equipped, so I ended up with badly pinched fingers.

When our children were young, Janice was blessed with an automatic washer, although we never had a clothes dryer. (We lived out in the country, and the God-given dryer of the sun and a gentle breeze gave our clothes the freshness and sweet scent that fabric softeners today can only pretend to imitate.) Wash day was no longer a day-long event every Monday. Now homemakers could sandwich a load here and there throughout the week, making it less of a drudgery.

And irons not only went electric, but they also added steam, and that made ironing less of a chore than it had been before. Even some of our clothes—especially my shirts and slacks, and Janice's dresses—came to be made of the new "permanent press," wrinkle-free fabric.

Janice's sewing machine was a wonder in itself. Not only could it sew, it could also zigzag and buttonhole. Repairing a hem was easy with it compared to using the old Singer powered by Grandma's feet.

Brooms were revolutionized, too. At first they were still made of straw, and just mass-produced. Then came the widespread use of synthetics and the bristles became more durable and more efficient. For millions of homemakers like my dear wife, Janice, vacuums made sweeping the carpets a breeze—well, at least more of a breeze than it had been.

Mother's little helpers didn't eliminate the cleaning of clothes and home, but they sure made the process a lot more bearable.

—Ken Tate

The Washing Machine

By Drid Williams

The Washington Street house in Baker, Ore., where my parents lived when I was born, was huge. By all accounts and old photographs, it was a grand old house: two stories with high-ceiling rooms, and at least three bedrooms upstairs. It had a staircase, a separate dining room, kitchen, "front room" (as it was called), and bathrooms upstairs and down.

It also had a full basement and a back porch. That's where the washing machine was kept.

Our all-metal Maytag, with four legs on casters for easy moving, was a metallic, silvery light green. Its round barrel housed a central pyramid-shaped mechanism that sloshed the clothes around under a removable lid. Sometimes Mama took the lid off while the clothes were washing and lifted me in her arms so I could see how the machine worked.

I watched, fascinated, as the blade turned almost all the way around, then back on itself, again and again. The engine hummed higher when the blade turned one direction and lower when it reversed. Even though I couldn't see the engine, I could hear it.

Underneath the machine, a spigot with a hose attachment was hooked on one side of the

barrel. That's how the dirty water ran out when the clothes were done. Another hose was connected to a single faucet on the heavy laundry tub hanging on the outside kitchen wall.

The first thing Mama did was turn on the clean water. Then she added dirty clothes and soap powder.

Our machine was luxuriously equipped with a wringer. Mama didn't have to turn a handle to make it work like Grandma did. When Mama finished washing, she let the dirty water out of the machine and turned the wringer on so she could feed the clean clothes, piece by piece, through the hard rubber rollers and into the laundry tub. Sometimes she rinsed the clothes a second time in the laundry tub, squeezing them through the wringer again.

To me, everything associated with the machine was consistently positive. Washing clothes every Monday morning was a familiar, homely act (as was ironing every Tuesday). Mama insisted that I play on the back porch while she worked so she could keep an eye on me. Even if she went inside, she could still see me through the screen door.

In winter, I played on the kitchen floor with my blocks and coloring books, but if I wanted, I could still watch Mama and the machine by standing in the open doorway (although she always complained that I let heat out of the house).

These circumstances infused our back porch and the washing machine with an aura of comfort, safety and well-being. That's why, when summer storms invaded Baker Valley, I ran for the back porch.

When lightning cracked the dark skies open and thunder grumbled and boomed, I crouched beneath the washing machine—my fortress of safety in an otherwise terrifying world. From there I could safely watch the weather's display, imagining the mighty game that was going on around us all.

I knew the gods were playing a game up there. Daddy had said they liked to bowl; that's what made the thunder.

And I could always tell when Thor bowled a strike because there was lightning. ❖

It'll All Come Out In the Wash!

The earliest way people cleaned clothes was by beating them against rocks and washing them in streams. Then the most rudimentary of clothes-washing tools—the scrub board—was invented in the late 18th century. Western civilization was headed down the road toward laundromatic revolution. The first machine designed for use in the home was built by William Blackstone of Bluffton, Ind., in 1874. Blackstone built the hand-powered machine for his wife as a birthday gift. Word spread of Blackstone's invention, and he began to build and sell washers for $2.50 each.

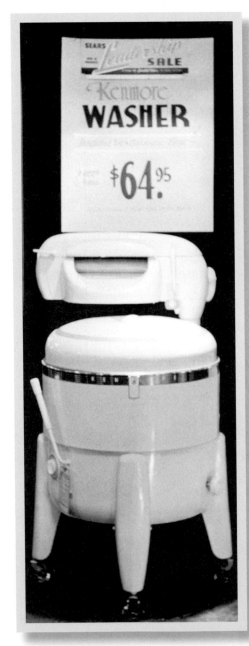

Within five years, Blackstone moved his company to Jamestown, N.Y., where it still operates today.

Many of us remember the early electric machines like the wringer washer at left, photographed in a Sears, Roebuck & Co. store in Syracuse, N.Y., in 1941. The standard movable wringer allowed laundry to be wrung once from the washer to a rinse tub and then again from the rinse to a basket headed for the clothesline.

Maytag and Whirlpool are two of the most venerable names in washing machine production. F.L. Maytag began his business in 1893

Machine Clean: Washer Trivia

How far did we come in just over 150 years (from 1800 to 1950)? A long way, if you consider the following bits of trivia.

The scrub board was invented in 1797.

The rotary washing machine was patented in 1858 by Hamilton Smith.

The wringer was invented in 1861.

The first "electricity-powered" washing machine was introduced in 1908 by the Hurley Co., of Chicago.

The first top-loading automatic washer was on the market in 1947, introduced by a corporate predecessor of Whirlpool.

Sales of automatic washers didn't surpass those of wringer washers until 1953.

"YOU SAVE AND SAVE AND SAVE with the new Westinghouse Laundromat" declares TV star Betty Furness, of Westinghouse STUDIO ONE. Miss Furness points out that the patented Weigh-to-Save Door actually is a scale that weighs each wash load. The indicator tells exact size of washing . . . and the exclusive Water Saver allows only the exact amount of water needed for that load (small, medium, regular) to be used. Result: Guesswork and waste are eliminated, and Laundromat users save up to 10 gallons of water a load.

SAVE 10 GALLONS OF WATER PER LOAD WITH WESTINGHOUSE NEW WAY TO WASH

LAUNDROMAT® New Patented Weigh-to-Save Door and Water Saver Take Guesswork out of Washing

Meet the new Westinghouse Laundromat . . . the automatic washer that saves 3 ways. It saves on soap and water. It saves wear and tear on clothes. And it saves countless hours of hard work and drudgery.

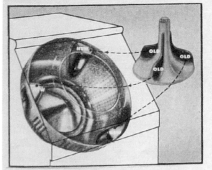

The Laundromat provides, too, a new and cleaner way to wash clothes. It eliminates the clumsy, old-fashioned agitator . . . and combines an advanced method of agitation for thorough cleaning, tumbling for gentleness, *and* lift-away action for rinsing. This new rinsing action equals 1,500 hand rinses . . . drains water and dirt *away* from clothes, not through them.

A comparison test will quickly prove that no other washer gives such dollars and cents savings as the new Laundromat . . . now being displayed and demonstrated at stores everywhere.

100% UNIFORM WASHING . . . Vanes are built right into washbasket (illustration, left) eliminating clumsy agitator and old center post that gave harsh, ineffective action. Clothes flush, lift, turn, tumble . . . 50 times a minute for completely uniform washing and rinsing.

IN YOUR NEW LAUNDROMAT, look for the free sample package of *all*—the new controlled-suds detergent. *all* is tested and approved by the Westinghouse Home Economics Institute for use in the Laundromat.

"OUT WITH THE OLD, IN WITH THE NEW... the Laundromat New Way to Wash!" says Betty Furness. "But get proof . . . see for yourself that the new Laundromat does save water, soap and money. See an actual demonstration at your dealer's! Too, you'll want to see the Laundromat's matching twin—the Westinghouse Electric Dryer—with its new way to dry clothes by patented direct air flow system that dries faster, at less cost . . . and cuts ironing time in half!"

FREE! Handsome Salt and Pepper Set. Plastic miniatures of famous Westinghouse Laundry Twins that are demonstrated by Betty Furness on Westinghouse STUDIO ONE and The BEST of BROADWAY. A Salt and Pepper set is yours free for seeing a demonstration of Laundromat New Way to Wash at your Westinghouse dealer's!

OWN THE NEW LAUNDROMAT FOR AS LITTLE AS $3.15 A WEEK

YOU CAN BE SURE...IF IT'S Westinghouse

Westinghouse Electric Corporation • Electric Appliance Division • Mansfield, Ohio

in Newton, Iowa, manufacturing farm implements. He added a washing machine to his line of products in 1907; soon the company was building washers exclusively.

Whirlpool began business as Upton Machine Co., of St. Joseph, Mich., in 1911. The company proudly proclaimed that it produced "electricity-powered" wringer machines.

John W. Chamberlain invented a machine in the mid-1930s that washed, rinsed and extracted water from clothes in a cycle of operations. Still, it was after World War II before the first automatic washers found their way to the market.

In the mid-1950s, Tide rode the automatic washer wave, giving consumers a free box of detergent inside every new machine (left). Speed Queen was just one of the 25 manufacturers that cooperated with the "Tide came in it!" campaign featuring the detergent and the washer in the same ad.

The miracle of modern laundering was complete with the development of the clothes dryer (facing page).

Like the washer, the dryer was invented long before it became a household appliance. The earliest dryer, invented in England in the early 1800s, was a barrel-shaped metal drum with holes punched in it. The drum was turned by hand over a fire.

African-American inventor George T. Sampson was awarded one of the earliest patents for a dryer in 1892. The first electric clothes dryer appeared around 1915.

Like automatic washers, gas and electric dryers became popular in the mid-1950s, and many times were sold in matching washer-dryer sets.

Modern washers and dryers made good on the promises of manufacturers to free women from wash-day drudgery. Mondays would never seem so blue again! ❖

Machine Clean: Washer Trivia

Another popular way to wash clothes in the 1950s and '60s was the laundromat. It probably wasn't as fashionable as the PolyClean Laundry Center featured in the ad published in 1962 (below), but it still had a way of making wash day a social event.

The first "washateria" opened in Fort Worth, Texas, on April 18, 1934.

The concept catered to homemakers who didn't have electricity, ample water or space for their own washers and dryers. Laundromats flourished in the two decades that followed, and most small towns had one.

Modern history aside, some people believe that the forerunner of the modern Laundromat may have been a service opened in 1851 by a gold miner and a carpenter in California. Their business served the original forty-niners with a 12-shirt machine powered by donkeys.

Poly Clean*

COIN-OPERATED
DRYCLEANING
AND
LAUNDRY CENTER

©Whirlpool Corporation, 1962. All rights reserved.

THIS is the self-service store where you save money and time!

Attention Businessmen:
Poly Clean Centers offer an important new profit opportunity. We invite inquiry regarding the franchise. Up to 90% financing to those qualified.

Deliverance From the Flatiron

By Annabelle Scott Whobrey

Going … going … GONE!" the auctioneer cried at the farm sale. Women gathered around the young buyer and admired the antique. I was in no way impressed, because the object of their excitement was an old flatiron exactly like the one I had used as a bride.

That flatiron reminded me of the era of attacking wrinkles in my husband's overalls with a red-hot iron heated on an equally hot wood range! Surely it was some lady of my time who had invented those delightful wash-and-wear fabrics and liberated us from dreadful days of drudgery at the ironing board.

In the wintertime, the kitchen took on an atmosphere of coziness as I ironed those baskets full of clothes. But in the summer when the temperature hovered around 100—whew!

As a young wife, I coyly kept reminding my husband of an ad I had seen in my mama's magazine for a new-fangled flatiron. I dreamt of owning an iron that I could use in a cooler place. I got little response to my hints until one day, my husband went to a farm sale to bid on a big work mule. Various things sold, and among the items was a self-heating iron like I'd seen in Mama's magazine. I suspected I got the iron because he felt guilty about the money he spent on his mule! I never questioned his motive, but happily hurled my old iron onto the heap of broken plow points, harrow teeth and other implements that were no longer useful.

Now I no longer needed a fire in the stove to heat my iron. A small flame fed by a tiny tank atop the iron was the source of heat. It didn't use much white gasoline, but it took oodles of air! I had to loosen a valve with wire pliers and apply the air with a pump. This little detail was almost the undoing of a very good marriage—OURS!

Those old enough to remember farming during the Depression will readily recall that it was absolutely necessary to take baling wire and pliers to the field for on-the-spot repairs. Parts and repair shops were too far away and too expensive, so farm folk made do with ingenuity and intestinal fortitude—and an ample

Deliverance from the heat of summertime ironing was first achieved with the gasoline-powered flatiron. It was advertised to heat for five hours on one cent's worth of gasoline.

Two-of-a-kind!

that make play of ironing

PROCTOR MOTHER-DAUGHTER

Gift Special

Mary Proctor Hi-Lo® Adjustable **IRONING TABLE**

and the *Miss* **Mary Proctor Hi-Lo®** Adjustable **IRONING TABLE**

LOOK, LITTLE MISS . . . Have your Mommy buy a Proctor Ironing Table and get one that works just like hers for yourself.

Full-Size Table, regularly **$14.95**

Tot's Table, with pad and cover, regularly **4.95**

Value **$19.90**

Both for $16.95

Mom's side of this bargain is the famous Mary Proctor Hi-Lo Ironing Table with more wife-saving features than any other ironing table in the world:

• It's always the right height for comfortable ironing — whether you sit or stand. Adjusts from 24″ to 36″ with fingertip control!

• Offset legs—plenty of room for freedom of the knees.

• No reaching ever towards ends—no need to get up—table rolls easily on wheels.

• Extra-wide, extra-long ironing surface.

• Can't wobble or tip because of its super-sturdy all-steel construction.

• Beautifully finished—in Proctor Gleaming White with chrome legs.

BUY NOW—IN TIME FOR CHRISTMAS

Montgomery Ward

Come, see—at your local Montgomery Ward's Retail Store —or your local Ward's Catalog Office.

IF NOT CONVENIENT, order from your nearest Ward Mail Order House—using catalog number 86-PWP-539R. Set will be shipped prepaid.

amount of baling wire and pliers. But now that I had my "new" iron, my husband had to share his pliers with me on ironing days and pray for no breakdowns! We were striving just to survive, and we had only one pair of pliers. This created a serious situation.

I vividly recall a beautiful April day when bees were buzzing, birds were building nests and Hubby was preparing ground for corn. I was humming *Springtime in the Rockies* as I finished the ironing. The precious pliers had been in my custody while my husband hoofed it behind the harrow.

Out in the yard, our young son was trying out his new tricycle. Doting grandparents had given him his first wheels and he was spinning them in the grass. It is a natural instinct for boys to practice being "shade-tree mechanics." I hadn't noticed when he'd borrowed our pliers. I only discovered that they were missing when

Hubby wanted to use them. A frantic search began! Spicy words were exchanged, unfit for our cute little culprit who was riding like crazy and oblivious to our argument.

Finally, somehow, I recalled our son's obsession with fixing his tricycle, and I asked him about the pliers. Quickly he was off and hunting in the tall grass. (Mercy no, we didn't have a lawn mower!) While we hunted, I made a resolution to save my egg money and buy my own pliers. The search ended on a silent note.

Today we can laugh about that crucial event. Actually, that old gasoline iron offered very little improvement for the person at the ironing board. When electricity came, it definitely was a deliverance from drudgery in most facets of farming.

No, I don't get nostalgic over an old sadiron. I wouldn't wish that method of ironing on an enemy, even if she owned her own pliers! ❖

A housewife and her little helper iron clothes side by side, circa 1955. Photo by Lambert, Getty Images.

Don't Lose Your Starch!

*I*f electricity helped us minimize the chores of ironing, one of the whiz-bang wonders of the 1960s held out an even greater promise: the elimination of ironing almost altogether!

Permanent press—also called "durable press"—was the new miracle treatment for shirts, blouses and slacks. In May 1962, a Manhattan shirt ad (left) asserted: "It irons in the wash!"   A proud husband bragged: "My wife iron? *Never*!"

Technically, permanent press is a process of fabric treatment that allows "flat drying, wet crease resistance" according to the patent granted in 1961 to the Deering-Milliken Research Corp.

Permanent press delivered freedom for professional and formal wear in the early 1960s. Thanks to permanent press and "self-ironing clothes," we no longer were worried about losing our starch. ❖

my wife iron? never!

This is no idle boast. I *mean* it. Now that I'm wearing Manhattan shirts of *Belfast*® self-ironing cotton she'll never have to iron again. *Belfast* cotton irons itself. Forever. Without touch-ups. Without long-winded washing instructions. Spin, hang or tumble dried, *Belfast* cotton washes cream-smooth every time. Stays smooth, soft and white all day long, as long as you wear it. Hint to wives: if you love to see your husband looking smart, but hate to iron, treat him (and yourself) to some new Spinsmooth Plus™ shirts of *Belfast* cotton by Manhattan. He'll like the way his shirts look. And you'll never have to iron again. Available in summer weight weaves in a wide selection of fashion collar styles. At fine stores everywhere. About $5.

Belfast®
self-ironing 100% cotton

IT IRONS IN THE WASH!

Manhattan®

Quality makers of the finest men's furnishings, sportswear and Lady Manhattan® *sportswear.*

New Broom Sweeps the Country

The *Perma-broom* with Electrene Bristles sweeps away dirt like lightning

Here's the *easiest way you ever knew* to get floors and rugs clean! It's so quick . . . so unbelievably thorough! A few easy strokes of the new Modglin **Perma-broom**, with its revolutionary Electrene Bristles, and dust and dirt disappear like magic!

Look for this colorful display in your store

Throw away that *obsolete* old-fashioned straw broom and get a Perma-broom at your grocer's today. Then watch dirt vanish!

Picks up dirt as it sweeps it off— Magnetic action of **Perma-broom's** Electrene Bristles picks up offending particles of lint, dirt, dog hairs and dust and sweeps them away.

Sudses clean in a jiffy—Swish your **Perma-broom** in warm water suds and shake it. Presto! It's sparkling clean and dry . . . with color as fresh and bright as the day you bought it!

Cleaning Up the Joint!

Whiz-bang wonders were springing up all over the house, particularly when it came to cleaning up the joint.

Cleaning up wasn't enough, either. We wanted to keep the home spotless without sacrificing soft skin and immaculate nails.

The colorful Perma-Broom swept the country in 1949

When you buy a Perma-broom . . . get its companion, the amazing **WHISK-OFF**

UTILITY SIZE

PURSE

with its Electrene bristles that swept away dirt like lightning. The new broom was much more efficient than the old straw standby and was easy to clean.

All of that and stylish, too!

"O-Cedar makes your life easier!" was the jingle for the new, "revolutionary" sponge mop that was introduced in the early 1950s.

No more wringing a mop out by hand, or using a bulky mop bucket. We could keep our hands out of soapy, dirty scrub water using the built-in squeezer.

Playtex Living Gloves were a new way to protect our hands from harsh chemicals used in cleaning—or from the daily task of washing dishes, for that matter. And they were available in two glamorous colors!

The claim that the gloves could "give you lovelier hands in only nine days" was enough to entice millions of housewives to use the new product.

The Playtex gloves obviously had staying power; the product recently celebrated its 50th anniversary.

With these and so many other new wonders on the market, it's no wonder it was easy to clean up the joint! ❖

Stop This Dirty Work!

Keep Hands Dry

Let O-Cedar's famous Sponge Mop keep your hands out of dirty scrub water. No more wringing—no wet hands. You simply press the water out with the handy built-in squeezer and your hands stay dry.

Save Mopping Time

O-Cedar's Sponge Mop, with its exclusive "wonder working angle," scrubs out stubborn dirt faster and gets in the corners too. Leaves the floor dry enough to wax or walk on only minutes after mopping.

Proved in use by more than 5 million women!

Revolutionary O-Cedar Sponge Mop

GUARANTEED FOR 5 YEARS

Sponge refills are available at $1.49 each. Buy several and have a separate head for waxing and special cleaning chores.

$3.95 COMPLETE

Guaranteed by Good Housekeeping

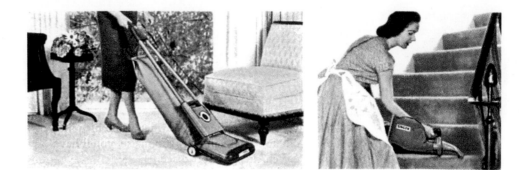

Happier With a Hoover

V acuuming the carpet certainly got a lot easier in the years between the introduction of the first "portable" vacuum cleaner in 1905—a 95-pound monster— and the 1950s.

Steadily, vacuums became lighter and more powerful. They featured more and more attachments and added disposable paper bags. Some of the fancier models even featured headlights.

All of that began with the invention of the first domestic, single-operator, upright vacuum cleaner by James Murray Spangler in 1907.

Spangler sold one of his first products to a cousin whose husband was Herbert H. Hoover.

Hoover later became president of the Hoover Co., with Spangler as his superintendent. The Hoover brand came to be synonymous with vacuums, and eventually there was a Hoover cleaner in most American homes.

Remember the beater bar on some of the early vacuum cleaners? The concept was to whack the carpet, causing dust to fly up and be captured in the suction and brushes of the sweeper. The beater bar on the Hoover vacuum engendered its own

You'll be happier with a HOOVER

(Whichever type you prefer)

Model 50 (*at right*). Hoover's great new cylinder cleaner. Most convenient cleaner of its type to use. Cleans by powerful suction. Features the exclusive new Dirt Ejector. Complete with cleaning tools in handy kit, Mothimizer, sprayer. **$79.50**

Model 28 (*at left*). Hoover's popular-priced Triple-Action Cleaner, with exclusive Hoover principle—it beats, as it sweeps, as it cleans. Converts instantly to an above-the-floor cleaner **$74.95**
Cleaning tools in handy kit, $19.95

What does a Hoover Cleaner do to make you happier? It gets more dirt wherever dirt is. It's easier to use, prolongs rug life and keeps colors bright. It offers you a complete choice of basic types and models to suit your cleaning needs and preference. It's the name everyone knows is best, preferred 2 to 1 over any other make. What are you waiting for?

Get happier today

Call your Hoover dealer for a home showing of the model you prefer.
THE HOOVER COMPANY, *North Canton, Ohio; Hamilton, Ont., Canada; Perivale, England*

Model 115 (*at right*). *Hoover, Junior. Ideal for small homes, handy for all homes. Cleans far bigger than its size. Stores in small space. Has Hoover's exclusive Triple Action—it beats, as it sweeps, as it cleans.*
$59.95
Cleaning tools extra.

slogan: "It beats as it sweeps as it cleans."

In England, Hoovers became so common-place that homemakers didn't say they were vacuuming—instead they were "hoovering."

By the 1950s and 1960s, manufacturers like Rainbow, Royal, Singer, Eureka and, of course, Hoover were providing upright and canister models with more and more attachments.

The ultimate in portability was introduced in handheld models.

The first disposable paper bags were used in 1955. The next year Hoover debuted the Constellation, a space-age concept that floated like a hovercraft on a cushion of air.

And, as modern carpeting diversified (shags, berbers, weaves, indoor-outdoor), the first height adjuster on upright cleaners was an innovation of 1970.

When it came to carpet sweeping, vacuuming wonders left us all happier with a Hoover—or any of the popular brands, for that matter. ❖

Life in a Vacuum

Carpet sweepers were introduced in the United States in 1858. There was no suction; cleaning was accomplished by a rotating brush powered by the wheels as the sweeper was pushed.

The first suction cleaner—although still non-electric—was the Whirlwind, manufactured in 1869 by the American Carpet Cleaning Co.

The first "portable" electric vacuum, invented in 1905, weighed 95 pounds and had a fan 18 inches in diameter to produce the suction. Needless to say, it didn't sell very well.

Hoover made the first vacuum to use both a cloth filter bag and cleaning attachments. The Model O was introduced in 1908 and weighed only 40 pounds.

The first convertible upright vacuums were introduced in the 1950s, and the first self-propelled models were manufactured in 1969.

❖❖❖

Early Vacuum Cleaners

By Jerry Haden

Back in the 1940s when I was growing up, most people who owned a vacuum cleaner probably had purchased it 20 years earlier. If it still did the job, why replace it? These vacuum cleaners from the 1920s and '30s were made of metal. They were heavy and, therefore, very durable.

As a child, I was fascinated by these cleaning machines. When my parents and I went to visit friends, the host would bring out the vacuum cleaner for me to inspect and perhaps operate.

My childhood fascination has stayed with me. Now, as an adult, I find that collecting these ancient vacuums makes an interesting hobby. Some of the early brand names are still in existence today: Royal, Hoover, General Electric, Eureka, Bissell. Other once-popular names, such as Apex, Premiere, Duplex and National, are unknown today.

Early vacuum sweepers were met with suspicion and downright hostility. All that suction power was thought to be dangerous! But housewives soon learned that vacuum cleaners were wonderful machines.

The oldest in my collection is a 1907 Regina pump. It takes two people to operate this model, one to pump and the other to run the nozzle along the carpet. Other vacuum cleaners on this order operate with only one person. The smallest vacuum in my collection is a child's toy, a 1925 Hoover.

My collection numbers about 25 now. However, I still keep on the lookout for older, different types that I don't have.

These old vacuum cleaners aren't worth a great deal of money, but who knows? Someday they could be. ❖

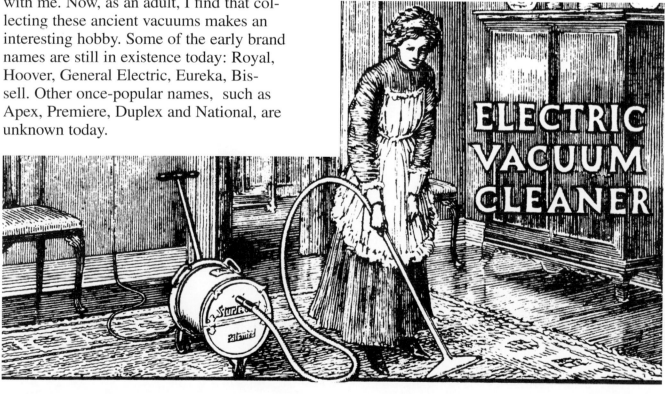

ELECTRIC VACUUM CLEANER

Pedal Power for Peace

By Barbara Davis

Grandmom's shiny black Singer sewing machine marched off to war in 1942. After years of making baby clothes, party dresses and living room drapes, the faithful Singer treadle sewing machine was recruited for the war effort—along with Grandmom.

Hoping to do something useful for the men in the military, a group of neighborhood ladies in Philadelphia formed a sewing circle and volunteered a couple of days every week working for the American Red Cross. These skillful seamstresses invaded a corner of the basement in the Henry W. Lawton Elementary School where they set up camp and proceeded to pedal for peace. Grandmom's Singer was loaded onto my wagon and pulled up the street to join the rest of the "troops" for the duration of the war.

One of Grandmom's biggest projects was sewing slippers for the wounded recuperating in military hospitals. She used a pattern to cut the sole and top portion of the slipper, and one size fit all! I can still feel the fabric she used: a bit like velvet, but much more durable. There were only two color choices—maroon and blue-gray. One day, she brought some of the scraps home for me, and I made wall-to-wall carpeting for my dollhouse. Nothing was ever wasted during the war.

While Grandmom was busy sewing for the American Red Cross, my father was away someplace with the Army. Mother got a job in a defense plant and Grandpop volunteered as an air-raid warden. Mother and I were the only ones who didn't get to wear a uniform, and I was unhappy about that.

However, I found a special duty to perform. It was my job to wash out the empty tin cans after dinner, place the top and bottom tin circles together inside the can, and then jump on it with all of my 40 pounds. Once the cans were flattened, I carried them up the street to the big red, white and blue 55-gallon drum on the corner where I dumped them for the weekly scrap-metal collection.

Back at the schoolhouse, it seemed like a million pairs of slippers had been made by those Red Cross volunteers and volunteers all over the world. I could just imagine the wounded soldiers shuffling around in Grandmom's slippers. The pedal power of those neighborhood ladies in the basement of the school during the hard years of World War II earned them a special citation from the British ambassador. Grandmom was very proud.

When the boys came marching home at the end of the war, the once-shiny Singer was retired with honor.

It was replaced in Grandmom's sewing room by a brand-new electric model—and yes, it was another Singer. ❖

Dreaming of a **WHITE** Christmas!

Fads & Fantasies

Chapter Four

Nothing is more "whiz-bang" than the fads and fantasies of the 1950s. I suppose some would argue that fads have been around forever and that there were similar phenomena in the Roaring Twenties.

I still think there has been no era in history so filled with fads and fantasies. The sheer number of Baby Boom youngsters reaching adolescence in the mid-1950s—and the huge expansion of radio, television and movies targeting that burgeoning part of the populace—ensured that our children knew what was hot and what was not.

Dolls have long been a favorite of little girls, but the 1950s saw the age of the Barbie and Ken phenomenon. Now it wasn't enough to have the doll—you also had to accessorize! There were lots of different outfits for all of the characters. There were wigs, sports gear and carrying cases that looked like miniature dressing rooms.

Playing house became a more involved game. Little girls still used refrigerator boxes for their playhouses, but now there were full miniature sets of china, and a dining table and chairs—with a tablecloth, no less. And not only that, but several of the play stoves of the 1950s had ovens that really worked, and real cookies came from them.

Then there were Hula Hoops, the craze that seemed to go hand-in-glove with the emergence of rock 'n' roll in the 1950s. My daughters both were able to twirl the Hula Hoop expertly—and both giggled heartlessly at my vain attempts to master the art myself!

What all-American boy did not want a coonskin cap after Walt Disney's Davy Crockett craze took ahold of the country? Who wouldn't want to be like the "King of the Wild Frontier"?

Other fads of the day grabbed our children's attention also. Boys and girls alike loved the Slinky and marveled at its ability to walk down stairs. And don't forget about the re-emergence of the yo-yo—one of the most transgenerational toys of all time—as a favorite plaything and pastime.

Yes, the fads and fantasies of those whiz-bang years were what molded the landscape of life for millions of our youngsters back in the Good Old Days.

—Ken Tate

A Doll For the Ages

arbie and Ken are more than the brainchildren of Elliot and Ruth Handler. They are their real children, too. But we're getting way ahead of the story. Let's start at the beginning of the Handlers' two families.

Elliot and Ruth were sweethearts in high school who went on to be sweethearts forever. Young and ambitious, the Handlers owned a company that made picture frames in the mid-1940s. Elliot and their partner, Harold Mattson, built the sample wooden frames while Ruth did the marketing.

Elliot began using scraps of leftover wood from the frames to make doll furniture. It was the beginning of a toy venture that ended up being a success beyond their dreams.

In 1945, the partners founded a company, Mattel—*Matt* from Harold's last name and *el* from Elliot's first.

Ruth was inspired to create Barbie as she watched her daughter and her daughter's friends play with paper dolls, popular in the 1950s. The girls made up adult or teenage roles for their dolls, pretending they were college students or adults with careers.

In the mid-1950s, while on a trip to Switzerland, Ruth bought a German doll named Lilli. Unlike almost all American dolls, Lilli was a grown-up.

Returning to the United States, Ruth went to work with Mattel's engineers and technicians on the design of the doll that would revolutionize toy-making.

Unlike baby dolls that had been popular with little girls for so long, or one-dimensional paper dolls, Barbie was modern and fashionable. At 11½ inches, Barbie was shapely, beautiful and cosmopolitan. Ruth even hired Charlotte Johnson, a clothing designer, and, over the years, they created a complete line of fashions for almost every occasion. From school to work to play to bed, Barbie did it all—and had an appropriate outfit as well.

All that was left was selecting a name. That

was easy. Elliot and Ruth named her Barbie, after their own daughter, Barbara. A few years later, in 1961, Barbie® doll's boyfriend joined the family, named Ken after the Handlers' son.

Mattel received a patent for Barbie in 1958, and in 1959 the Handlers and Mattel took their new creation to the New York Toy Show. The reception was rather cool, and the new doll was viewed as a risky investment in store display space.

But once Barbie made it to toy-department shelves, the public loved her. By 1960, Mattel couldn't keep up with the demand.

Customers bought around $500 million in Barbie products by 1970. The rest, as they say, is history.

No product better reflected the fads and fantasies of little girls of the whiz-bang years. ❖

Doll in the Window

By Mary Farmer

The doll was in the corner grocer's window. Each time before I entered the store with list in hand, I would stand and stare longingly at her pink-cheeked face, her soft brown eyes and dark lashes and, most appealing, her pretty mouth with the two white teeth showing. She wore a pink dress with matching socks and Mary Jane shoes.

Part of me said she cost too much for my parents to buy her for me. But a diligent part of me went on dreaming.

As my 8th birthday approached, my mom told me that she would give me a party and that I could invite my friends. It was my first party. May 27 was a week away. I had invited seven neighborhood girls, three of whom I rarely played with. I spent every afternoon after school standing in front of the grocery store window. I was telling myself that if my parents could make a party for me despite struggling during the Depression to raise my brothers and me, then maybe they would buy the wonderful doll for me. On Saturday, while Mom was at the market and Papa was sawing wood with a neighbor in the back yard and my brothers were out playing somewhere, I sneaked into the closet where I guessed my presents would be hidden.

She Wets and Weeps and Blows Her Nose!
BETSY WETSY

Made of lifetime vinyl—not rubber. Will not pick up dirt. Magic skin wipes clean with a damp cloth, so she keeps her fresh, baby-pink complexion for life. Ideal process completely eliminates seams. Layette includes slip, dress, bonnet. $9.98.

IDEAL TOY CORPORATION
200 Fifth Ave., New York 10, N. Y.

GIFT FOR:_____

She smiles! She pouts! Only Ideal's
MAGIC LIPS DOLL
changes expression for you!

You can make her lips move and control her expression to smile or pout. Only Ideal's Magic Lips doll has this exclusive crying and lip-moving feature. Comes with her own toothbrush to care for her very own baby teeth. Saran wig can be washed, shampooed, combed. $14.98.

IDEAL TOY CORPORATION
200 Fifth Ave., New York 10, N. Y.

GIFT FOR:_____

Betsy Wetsy and the Magic Lips Doll were two of Ideal Toy's best-known offerings in the Christmas toy section of Life magazine's Nov. 28, 1955, issue. Note the "Gift For" line. The section became a wish list for Santa's little helpers.

Santa Brought Dolls

By Hazel Gray Miller

My sister and I received dolls for Christmas during our childhood years. I did not get dolls for other occasions, but I do remember a cloth doll Mother made for me from an old sock. He was dressed in overalls, but he had no arms because when I came into the house and found Mom making the doll, I wouldn't wait for her to attach arms.

My doll had crooked button eyes and a grinning embroidered mouth. I called him Frankie after a man who helped my Grandpa plow and plant his fields.

Frankie tipped the bottle when he was working, and he squinted and twisted his mouth as he sang songs in Swedish. I thought my doll looked like him.

We had big Peggy dolls that cried "Mama!" when we turned them over. These dolls had composition heads, arms and legs, and stuffed bodies. I also remember smaller composition dolls dressed in knitted snowsuits.

In 1936, my sister, Gale, and I got composition drink-and-wet dolls. Santa brought these dolls in little cardboard suitcases. They were dressed in organdy dresses, and came with diapers and tiny baby bottles. I named my doll Janie after Jane in my *Dick and Jane* reader.

We had Susan dolls that wore ice skates and wore their hair in braids. Santa also brought a soldier doll for my sister, and I had a sailor doll. I named him LaJune, after a Canadian sailor my dad had met. Dad liked him so much that when my sister was born, my parents gave her the middle name LaJune.

The last childhood doll I received was in 1942, when my dad purchased Magic Skin dolls from Firestone. The dolls were dressed in organdy. Their heads were hard, but soft latex Magic Skin covered their arms and legs.

Today I collect dolls, and I try to find dolls like those from my childhood.

I have never seen Susan dolls or Magic Skin dolls like the ones we had. As for Frankie, he was one of a kind. ❖

I found paper plates, crepe paper and hats, but no big box like the one in which the beautiful doll would come. There was something wrapped in tissue paper. Carefully I opened it. Inside was a doll—but it was a homemade doll, crudely sewn. My heart sank. Numbly, I rewrapped it.

At the party, I pretended to be surprised when Mom handed me her doll. However, I know my disappointment must have shown all too well.

My other presents included several boxes of handkerchiefs, a comb-and-brush set, and a box of chocolates. The three girls I hardly knew ate most of those. I never wanted a party after that.

I don't know what happened to that homemade doll. I may have played with it.

I just don't remember.

Many years later, I was at a church craft sale and stopped at a table—and there was a homemade doll. Looking at it, I was overcome by a rush of emotion. It was a lot like the one my mom had made for me. I quickly bought it.

Driving home with the doll on the seat beside me, I blinked away tears.

I realized now how much love my mom had sewn into that crude doll she had made, no doubt during the hours when I was asleep, even though she must have been tired from her long hours of work at the factory. ❖

Stairing Down Success

Sometimes inspiration just springs into an inventor's mind. In 1943, Richard James, a naval engineer, was working to develop a meter for battleships. A tension spring he was working with was accidently knocked from his work bench, and Richard watched as it kept moving after hitting the floor.

Boing! The inspiration bounced into Richard's mind for what would become the Slinky.

Richard told his wife, Betty about the idea. The couple spent the next two years working out the details of manufacturing and marketing their invention. Richard developed equipment to turn 80 feet of steel wire into each Slinky.

Betty came up with the name, choosing Slinky because of its dictionary meaning of "sleek or sinuous."

The new toy was demonstrated during the 1945 Christmas season at Gimbel's Department Store in Philadelphia, and the Jameses sold 400 Slinkys in the 90-minute demonstration.

Buoyed by their success, they founded James Spring & Wire Co., renamed James Industries in 1956.

The new toy caught on almost immediately, and remains popular even today. The company estimates that more than 250 million Slinkys have been sold worldwide.

Betty took over as CEO of the company in 1960 and moved production to Hollidaysburg, Pa., where Slinkys are still produced today using the original equipment designed by Richard, who died in 1974.

Poof Toys bought the Slinky brand in 1998. Betty James was inducted into the Toy Industry Hall of Fame in 2001. ❖

A TV Jingle Classic

It's Slinky received its first exposure in 1963. Composed for a television commercial, the jingle featured the sound of a Slinky walking down stairs to the beat of the music. The jingle has been on television longer than any other, and has been translated into several languages.

Do you remember how *It's Slinky* went?

What walks down stairs, alone or in pairs,
And makes a slinkity sound?
A spring, a spring—a marvelous thing.
Everyone knows it's Slinky!
It's Slinky! It's Slinky!
For fun it's a wonderful toy.
It's Slinky! It's Slinky!
It's fun for a girl and a boy!

Doing the Hula Hoop!

*I*f you were a youngster living in Southern California in 1958, you might have noticed an odd pair on your playground demonstrating a new toy.

They were Richard Knerr and Arthur "Spud" Melin, and the toy they had reinvented and renamed was the Hula Hoop.

Richard and Spud had founded the Wham-O Co. in 1948 and had been looking for a product with which to break through.

The inspiration came in 1957 from an acquaintance who had visited Australia and told the two entrepreneurs about children twirling bamboo hoops around their waists in gym class.

Knerr and Melin experimented with toys themselves and often tried them out directly on potential buyers. After a few months with the Hula Hoops on the playgrounds, they knew they had a hit.

Wham-O sold more than 100 million Hula Hoops in the first two years of production. The Hula Hoop is now widely recognized as the biggest and most profitable fad of the 1950s. ❖

A bobby-soxer demonstrates the Hula Hoop in 1957.
Photo by Keystone, Getty Images.

Coonskin Craze

*B*orn on a mountaintop in Tennessee,
The greenest state in the land of the free,
Raised in the woods so's he knew ev'ry tree,
Kilt him a b'ar when he was only three.
Davy, Davy Crockett! King of the wild frontier!
So went the first verse to *The Ballad of Davy Crockett,* written for the 1955 classic Walt Disney production of *Davy Crockett.* Who would have suspected that the story of a frontier hero from the 19th century would start one of the biggest crazes of the 1950s?

Even Walt Disney himself had no idea of the stir that would be created when, just before Christmas 1954, *Disneyland* (the original name of the television program) aired the first of three Davy Crockett adventures.

The Crockett craze spread like wildfire on a frontier prairie. Actor Fess Parker captured a unique blend of history, legend and—most importantly—down-home likeability in the title role.

Buddy Ebsen (later Jed Clampett in television's 1960s *The Beverly Hillbillies*) added a comic element to the show.

By the time the second installment of the Crockett series aired the following January, the whole country—and particularly our little boys—had gone crazy for all things Crockett.

Facing page: Fess Parker strides through the frontier as Davy Crockett. The photograph was taken in 1955 at the height of the coonskin craze. Photo by Allan Grant, Time Life Pictures/Getty Images.

Left: A youngster, surrounded by Davy Crockett books and wearing a T-shirt adorned with his hero, tries on a coonskin cap for the first time. Photo by John Dominus, Time Life Pictures/Getty Images.

Crockett mania extended to books, lunch boxes, wallets and clothing. And the recording of *The Ballad of Davy Crockett* sold 10 million records within a year!

The third installment of the series, "Davy Crockett at the Alamo," aired Feb. 14, 1955. That took the story of Davy to the heroic stand at San Antonio, but the public clamored for more, and Walt Disney wasn't one to ignore public opinion.

A new, two-episode show, *Davy Crockett and the River Pirates*, was on production even as the original series, edited for theatrical release, moved to the big screens in May 1955.

Davy Crockett and the River Pirates aired on *Disneyland* in November and December 1955; like the original program, *Davy Crockett and the River Pirates* was edited and released in theaters the next year.

The coonskin craze enjoyed a renaissance—although not nearly as dramatic as the 1950s fad—when Fess Parker returned to the small screen as Daniel Boone in the 1960s.

For millions of Baby Boom boys and their parents, the frontiersman fad and fantasy is one of the most enduring and endearing of the Good Old Days. ❖

Foremost, there was the huge demand for coonskin caps. Untold millions were sold in the first year of the fad. If you were a little boy and you didn't have a coonskin cap, you felt just plumb left out!

But the cap was just the tip of the proverbial iceberg. There were Davy Crockett cork guns. Little frontiersmen lined up in skirmishes all over their make-believe Tennessee. They practiced "grinnin' down a b'ar"—even if it was just an ornery big brother.

The World On a String

By John L. Patton

Almost every day was special for a youngster growing up in the Cincinnati, Ohio, neighborhood of Fairmount back in the late 1940s and '50s. Summers were filled with fun and games, and there were circus parades, Fourth of July picnics, and vendors of all sorts with horse-drawn carts. But perhaps the most special day of all was the day when the Duncan Yo-Yo Champions came to our neighborhood street corner.

The mid-1950s signaled the end of the Duncan Yo-Yo Champion era, so I never knew the full glory of it. But the program sure helped increase sales of Duncan Yo-Yos like nothing else could have. Every summer, probably since the mid-1930s, Duncan would hire men—and even some young women—from across the country who were yo-yo experts. Then Duncan would send them out in pairs into neighborhoods where they put on Duncan Yo-Yo demonstrations. Newspaper and radio ads promoted these live events two weeks in advance.

Boys and girls from 4-years-olds to teens saved their allowances in anticipation of that special day, which usually arrived on a Saturday. And these Duncan Yo-Yo Days lasted all day.

First the Duncan Yo-Yo Champions would give every boy and girl a pack of yo-yo string. (The string was the unwaxed kind, but hey, it was free!)

Then, while one of the Champions performed all the newest tricks, the other told us the history of the yo-yo. (It might have been only a story, but we were told that the yo-yo was originally a weapon.) They also told us all about the Duncan Yo-Yo factory, and they even had a nifty display of old Duncan Yo-Yos.

Then the fun was ready to begin. Using either Duncan Yo-Yos we already had, or one of the new models we had just bought, we all took part in yo-yo contests, divided into groups by age. The very best won

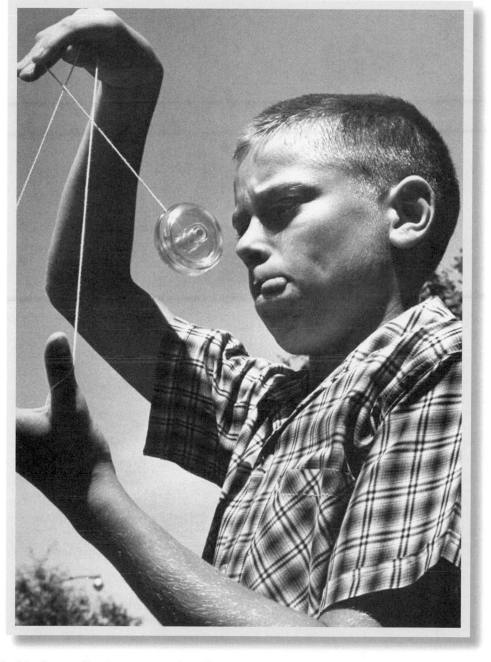

Deluxe Duncan Yo-Yos.

Even kids from the poorest families could afford to buy at least one yo-yo. Most of us, though, bought several models, or splurged on a Deluxe Duncan Yo-Yo.

But Duncan Yo-Yo also had another gimmick: the string.

They sold two kinds: a basic, inexpensive string, which sold three for a dime; and a special waxed one, which not only lasted longer but also helped you do more of the tricks of the trade; these sold two for 15 cents.

For weeks after Duncan Yo-Yo Day, all of us kids held our own competitions. Nearly every store that sold Duncan Yo-Yos stocked up on string and probably doubled their Duncan Yo-yo orders. And while we still played pinball and bought our soda pop and Cracker Jacks, most of our money and attention for the entire summer was focused on Duncan Yo-Yos.

Now, I was never very good with my Duncan Yo-Yo, but I still had fun trying. And if memory serves me, the most I ever paid for a genuine Duncan Yo-Yo was a quarter.

Out of curiosity, I searched the Internet to see if Duncan Yo-Yo is still in business.

Not only are they still in business, but their Web site at www.yo-yo.com offers both classic and updated models—and considering that 50 years have flown by, their prices are quite reasonable, or at least they seem so to me. I just might order a pair of the classics I played with as a boy, back in my own Good Old Days. That's when I had the world on a string. ❖

Toys! Toys! Toys!

*A*s the Baby Boom generation reached adolescence in the late 1940s and early 1950s, and as an expanding economy put memories of the Great Depression behind us, toymakers began to gear up.

Parents of the 1950s were making more money, and they were spending a lot of it on what a lot of them hadn't had when *they* were children: Toys! Toys! Toys!

Toy trains; Roy Rogers cowboy outfits, complete with holsters and six-shooters; bikes; wagons; real, working Singer sewing machines; dollhouses; playhouses—everything kids could imagine seemed to be on the shopping lists for birthdays and Christmas.

It was a heady time for toy manufacturers, too. Take, for example, the origin of the Frisbee.

The Frisbie Baking Co., of Bridgeport, Conn., made pies that were very popular with students at New England colleges during the Depression era. One day some unidentified students discovered that they could toss the tins from the Frisbie pies (above) back and forth.

In 1948, Walter Morrison and a partner invented a plastic version of the Frisbie pie tin. It was lighter and could fly farther with greater accuracy than the pie tins.

The partners split up before the product became successful, and Morrison went on to produce a plastic Frisbie called the Pluto Platter, hoping to cash in on public interest in UFOs.

Richard Knerr and "Spud" Melin of Wham-O fame first saw the Pluto Platter in late 1955. Morrison signed a deal with Wham-O (one that would net him over $1 million in royalties over the years), and the company began production of the product in January 1957.

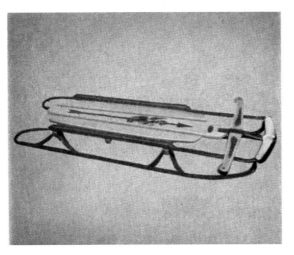

Two of the most popular toys during the whiz-bang years were the Flexible Flyer sled for winter (above) and the Thunderbird wagon for summer.

The next year, Frisbie Baking closed its doors and Knerr of Wham-O coined a variation on the name for the company's new product: the Frisbee.

Wham-O sold more than 100 million Frisbees before selling the brand to Mattel.

Today there are 20 or more makers of flying disks of various names. Untold numbers have been sold and given away as promotional gifts and premiums.

But the the original Frisbee will always be a toy close to the hearts of boys and girls from the whiz-bang years.

This little girl was so excited when she got her very own working model Singer sewing machine in 1955.

Banks were popular toys back in the whiz-bang years. Remember the Creepy Hand bank? It had a ghoulish hand that crept from a box, grasped a coin and yanked it inside.

Other popular banks played on the science fiction and space exploration angles, such as the bank below that rocketed the coin into a slot in the planet. Courtesy Rod Lautzenheiser, Berne, Ind.

Still other banks were premiums, like the Donald Duck bank from the 1940s (left) that was transformed from an empty Nash peanut butter jar.

DONALD DUCK BANK
COIN SLOT
Nash QUALITY
TRY DONALD DUCK PEANUT BUTTER

"Save With"
FIRST BANK OF BERNE
BERNE, INDIANA

Parents also looked for toys that would stretch their children's intellect. Board games had been popular throughout the 1920s and 1930s, and the trend continued into the whiz-bang years.

After World War II, Anthony Pratt designed the whodunnit game of *Clue*. Pratt and his wife came up with the idea for the game in 1944, but it was five years before they worked out the mysterious wrinkles, and before postwar shortages had eased so that production could begin.

Millions have now worked to solve the mystery of how and by whom Mr. Boddy was murdered. Perhaps it was Colonel Mustard with a knife in the kitchen. …

Parker Brothers bought rights to *Clue* in 1949. Today the game is sold in 40 countries.

The games we played in the 1950s included

many favorites from the 1930s, such as *Sorry* (first sold in 1934) and *Monopoly* (1935).

But there were new games on the market as well. Scrabble (see below) came out in 1952, followed by Yahtzee in 1956. The year 1959 was a good one for gaming. *Concentration*, *Risk* and *Diplomacy* were all introduced that year.

Perhaps it was a backlash to all the toys flooding the market.

Or perhaps it was just parents realizing that they needed to feed the minds of their children, and games—even educational ones—were not enough.

So it was only natural that publishers of encyclopedia and other educational books—like *The Children's Encyclopedia* (facing page)—asked parents, "Have you given them what they *really* need?"

It is no accident that the education that fueled the space race of the 1960s was born in the whiz-bang era of the Good Old Days. ❖

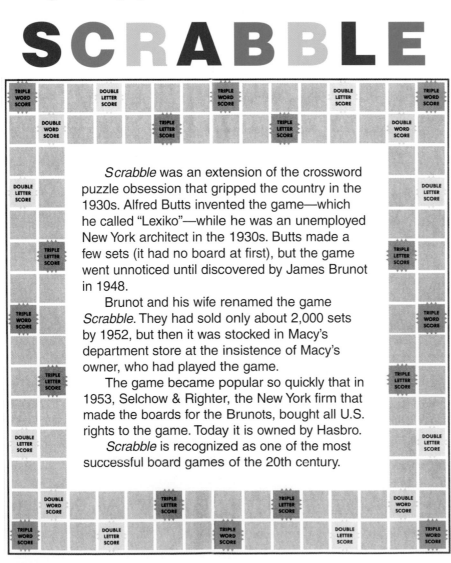

SCRABBLE

Scrabble was an extension of the crossword puzzle obsession that gripped the country in the 1930s. Alfred Butts invented the game—which he called "Lexiko"—while he was an unemployed New York architect in the 1930s. Butts made a few sets (it had no board at first), but the game went unnoticed until discovered by James Brunot in 1948.

Brunot and his wife renamed the game *Scrabble*. They had sold only about 2,000 sets by 1952, but then it was stocked in Macy's department store at the insistence of Macy's owner, who had played the game.

The game became popular so quickly that in 1953, Selchow & Righter, the New York firm that made the boards for the Brunots, bought all U.S. rights to the game. Today it is owned by Hasbro.

Scrabble is recognized as one of the most successful board games of the 20th century.

have you given them what they REALLY need?

for Christmas and a lifetime...

The shiny red bike, the varsity football, the hatbox just like Mom's...they're your way of telling your children "We love you." But youngsters need more than love alone if they are to become happy and successful adults. They need the thoughtful, intelligent atmosphere only **you** can give them...with the remarkable BOOK OF KNOWLEDGE.

CURIOSITY—THE GREAT TEACHER

Wonderful things happen when THE BOOK OF KNOWLEDGE comes into the home. Spurred on by curiosity, the child spends hours with his new-found treasure. He learns to find his own answers to every question, from art to atoms...learns to know great minds and be at ease with great ideas...discovers how to make and do things for himself...**and learns,**

above all, **that learning is fun.** The whole family comes to depend on these 20 volumes, with their 7,600 pages, their hundreds of delightfully written articles and their more than 13,000 pictures-that-teach.

ENRICHES THE CHILD'S LIFE

What a rich and rewarding environment for young minds to grow in! And what pride the parent feels... as he watches his child's interests expand, sees him develop the initiative and confidence that lead to a bright and happy future! Give your child the chance millions of others have had. **Give him** THE BOOK OF KNOWLEDGE, **the gift that lasts a lifetime.**

A FREE GIFT FOR YOUR CHILDREN

A new, exciting booklet the whole family will enjoy! 24 thrill-packed pages show you actual pages in

full color from the latest edition of THE BOOK OF KNOWLEDGE...with quizzes, nursery rhymes and games, questions and answers that will teach your child dozens of useful facts. Just mail the coupon for your child's copy. There is no obligation, of course.

CHRISTMAS BONUS IF YOU ACT NOW!

We will send you—**absolutely FREE**—a copy of "The Story of Santa Claus and Christmas Carols" **if your coupon reaches us by December 5th.** This colorful booklet tells the story of Santa Claus as it appears in THE BOOK OF KNOWLEDGE. In addition, it is packed with lovely, centuries-old Christmas carols and poems illustrated in color, to bring the real spirit of Christmas into your home. To be sure **your** child receives a copy, mail the coupon **today.**

THE BOOK OF KNOWLEDGE®

THE CHILDREN'S ENCYCLOPEDIA

First choice of parents for more than 40 years

FREE! *this delightful color booklet...*

© The Grolier Society Inc. 1955

Captain Midnight & the Decoder

By Pieter Mayer

For several months, every afternoon at 5:15 p.m., right after *Tom Mix*, I got my pencil and a piece of paper and sat down to listen carefully to what Pierre Andre, spokesman for the Midnight organization, would say at the end of that afternoon's radio program.

It was important to me, during those days after the second World War, to belong to Captain Midnight's Secret Squadron, and when the chance came to join, I was thrilled. The opportunity to join the Secret Squadron didn't come along all that often, so I had to pay attention to Mr. Andre. If I didn't, I might miss—as he'd often tell us—"the chance of a lifetime."

Then, one afternoon in late August, on the same day he captured his greatest nemesis, Ivan Shark, Captain Midnight himself spoke to

us. This was the first time since I'd started listening that the Captain had taken time from his busy schedule of fighting the powers of evil to speak to us personally. I sat there, my ear glued to the speaker. I knew this was going to be the big one! I knew the Captain was going to make me an offer I couldn't refuse!

He didn't disappoint me. In the same clear, deep voice he normally used on evildoers, he told us that a few privileged listeners were going to be offered Secret Squadron memberships. At that point, my sister came into the room and coughed. I told her to shut up or get out. My piece of paper was ready. My glasses sat firmly on the bridge of my nose. My pencil was sharp. Then Captain Midnight said that Pierre Andre was going to tell us how to join, right after "today's secret message" and a word from Ovaltine.

It was those secret messages that had given me the itch to enlist in the first place. I just couldn't decipher the darn things, and my friends who could wouldn't tell me one word of what they said. I knew that all my frustration would end if only I could have the captain's glow-in-the-dark, silent-dog-whistle, Secret Squadron decoder. *And now, at last*, I thought, *I'm going to own one!*

Pierre Andre thanked the captain for taking the time to talk to us. Then he gave us all the information we needed to get the decoder. I had to send in the label from a jar of Ovaltine (a beverage I wasn't crazy about, but which my sister was willing to drink), 50 cents taped to a piece of cardboard, and my name and address. (You could send coins taped to cardboard in those days and expect them to get where they were going.)

After several weeks, the decoder and my membership card arrived. I was thrilled. I tore open the package in front of my sister and mother. Holding up the decoder before them, I danced around the living room. It was clear that they hadn't been caught up in the moment, though, so I went to my room to enjoy the decoder in private.

I'd read that you could make the silent dog whistle work by blowing into the top of it. I blew as long and hard as I could, but my old beagle, Jinx, who'd been lying with his chin on my foot, didn't budge. So right there, I lost interest in the whistle.

Then I tried the decoder. I'd carefully taken down the secret message I'd heard the day I learned how to get the

The Captain Midnight decoder whistle mentioned in the story is pictured on the facing page. Captain Midnight wasn't only featured on radio. At right is a poster for Captain Midnight (1942), a movie based upon the radio serial. Then, from 1954–58, the Captain was featured in a television serial.

decoder. Each number of the code represented a letter of the alphabet; a 4, for instance, would be a "D," and a 25, a "Y."

It took me half an hour to figure it all out, and when I had, I was furious. The message read: "Drink Ovaltine every day." Well, for gosh sakes, I wasn't going to do *that!* Now I knew why no one had wanted to tell me about the messages they'd received. They were too embarrassed!

That left me with only one thing to look at, the decoder's best feature: the way it could glow in the dark. I had to hold the decoder an inch or so from a burning light bulb for a few seconds to charge it up. I did, burning the tips of my fingers slightly in the process. Then I took the decoder into my closet, closed the door behind me, and held it out in the pitch dark about a foot from the tip of my nose. It glowed a ghostly green for a little while, then faded away.

I left the closet, tossed the decoder into the pieces of ripped cardboard it had come in, and went to the top of the stairs. "Ma," I called down, "what's for dinner?" ❖

Right: The decoder silent dog whistle was just one of the premiums offered during the 10-year run of Captain Midnight on radio. Pictured here is the Captain Midnight Secret Squadron Decoder Badge.

Names After Midnight

Captain Midnight was known as Jet Jackson in Australia. There was already a Captain Midnight down under, and he was an outlaw!

After two seasons on television beginning in 1954, the series' title was changed to *Jet Jackson, Flying Commando* because Ovaltine, the ex-sponsor, owned rights to the *Captain Midnight* title. Soundtrack references to Captain Midnight were overdubbed for the rest of the series' four-year life.

Above: A Green Hornet secret compartment ring was a premium for that popular 1940s radio show.
Right: Not all hero-related toys were premiums. This Dan Dare walkie-talkie set from around 1955 also included a secret decoder. Dan Dare, Pilot of the Future was a comic that began in April 1950 in Eagle magazine, and continued weekly until the magazine ceased publication in 1969.
Hulton Archive/Getty Images

Ultimately, fads faded and our fantasies came back to real-world dreams. The Sears, Roebuck & Co. Wishbooks of the 1950s were filled with such reality-based fun. In 1956, Sears offered an all-metal doll house (above) that presented the American dream at its best—the real world mixed with some fantasy. What little boy (or little girl) wasn't lured by the romanticism of the rails. The American Flyer model train (left) was offered in the 1958 catalog. Merchandise featuring heroes like Roy Rogers and Dale Evans bridged the gap between real life and fantasy, and youngsters gobbled up items like the Roy Rogers pocket watch and stopwatch (below) offered in the mid-1950s.

Kurt Ard

Permanent Solutions

Chapter Five

*I*n the late 1950s and early 1960s, the idea of a woman having the time, money and inclination to visit a beauty salon was a socially acceptable concept. At first it was for special occasions: a high school prom or some other special date for a teenager, an anniversary or wedding for an adult.

Then the trips to the stylist became much more routine as we found more reasons to search for permanent solutions.

It hadn't always been like that. Up until the 1920s, women seldom cut their hair, and long, flowing locks were wound up and pinned neatly into tight coiffures. Then, in the Roaring Twenties, the most daring women bobbed their hair. Shorter hair ultimately was the boon of the salon, as women rushed to get cuts and curls at any price.

Little girls weren't left completely out of the picture, even in those early days. Many mothers dreamed that their daughters would become the next Shirley Temple and subjected the girls to electric curl machines or curling irons—anything to get the darling 'do of Shirley. Surely there was some way of curling even the straightest of hair!

The beauty shop didn't stop at the top, either. It offered complete facials, manicures and pedicures.

The beauty shop didn't stop at the top, either. It offered complete facials, manicures and pedicures. A woman coming to the salon for "the works" could leave feeling pampered. That was pretty special when you were reminded by the little buckaroo asleep on the salon couch beside you that the remainder of your day would be as hectic as your beauty appointment had been relaxing.

Permanent solutions weren't something a woman found only in the salon. The whiz-bang years saw the introduction of home beauty products by the hundreds.

The first home permanents and hair coloring products gave women the "do it yourself" spirit. Beauty soaps replaced homemade lye soap in the bathroom. Lipstick, nail polish and cologne all gave beautiful women the chance to feel and look even more beautiful.

Permanent solutions—whether in the salon or at home—were some of the most important whiz-bang wonders to women back in the Good Old Days.

—Ken Tate

Beauty Before Avon

By Phyllis C. Jordan

Recently I saw a television commercial that went into raptures over a shampoo that left the hair "fresh" for *two days!* It brought back memories of a summer day in the country at my grandmother's house. I was visiting her and preparing to wash my hair for a date. It was the middle of the week and I remarked that my boyfriend was special enough to deserve an extra shampoo, for I usually washed my hair on Saturdays.

"You wash your hair *every week?*" exclaimed Grandma. "Why, child, you'll *ruin* your hair! You'll take every bit of the shine and life out of it."

"It gets dirty and won't curl if I don't wash it often," I protested.

"That's just your imagination. Believe me, I've had hair longer than you have."

"How often do you wash yours, Grandma?"

"Sometimes not all winter. Wet hair can give you flu or bronchitis. I wash it several times in the summer, when it's hot. We used to take kettles of hot and cold water out in the back yard, my sisters and I, and pour it over each other's heads and then dry our hair in the sun.

OCTAGON SOAP.

Little Miss Octagon.

Rainwater is best to use on it, but sometimes it didn't rain much and we had to use well water. Even *that* was better than what you get in town."

"What kind of shampoo?" I persisted.

"We used plain old-fashioned yellow Octagon soap. There's nothing better. I don't care how fancy they've got."

Finally I persuaded her to pretend it was "used-to days" and join me in a hair wash out in the back yard. We heated several buckets of water in the reservoir on the woodstove. First we soaped our hair thoroughly in the kitchen sink, massaging the shampoo in well. Then we took a kettle each of warm and cold water out in the yard. First she poured the warm water over my head, then the cold. Warm water was better for taking the soap and dirt out, she said, but the cold water took out the tangles.

I got some more water and rinsed hers. Then we sat out in the sun, lazily combing our hair, and while it dried, we talked girl talk with many reminiscences. I had stayed with my grandparents often in the summer when I was a child (and sometimes in the winter, for my stepfather and I were oil and water—utterly incompatible).

I asked her if she remembered my experiment with makeup.

At first she smiled a little, but then she began to chuckle. My grandmother did not approve of cosmetics. She called them "paint," and was convinced that those who used them couldn't be "nice" women. If Grandma had a motto, it was "As is."

Her biggest concession was talcum powder for her face on Sunday. She called it "whitening," and it was just that—white. She was quick to point out that she was not trying to change the Lord's work in any way. It was just a matter of looking "decent for Church" (the capital letter was hers).

For the same reason, she put buttermilk on my freckles. When I ventured to ask if the Lord hadn't made my freckles, she answered sharply, "Indeed not! They're from your carelessness, running around in the sun without anything on your head." A white complexion was a mark of beauty in Grandma's day and she shook her head in disbelief at those who deliberately tried to tan their skins.

Until I was 12, I cared little about how I looked. I had known all my life that my cousins were the beauties, and there really wasn't much use losing sleep over it.

Then, all at once, I cared. I was miserable that my hair was straight, that I freckled easily, that I was scrawny. Grandma's ideal girl was curly haired, dimpled, pink and white.

That coupon in the magazine was meant just for me. For only a quarter, one could get a generous sample of a company's beautifiers—Lady Esther's, I think. I extracted the necessary coin from my metal bank. I didn't want to ask for it because I intended it to be a glorious surprise. I filled out the coupon, knowing that at last I, too, could be beautiful. I waited at the gate for the mailman every day for three weeks, and on the lucky day, I ran upstairs fast enough to make Mr. Guinness' list.

The box was plain cardboard and fitted with holes that contained a miniature jar of cream, a small box of pink powder, and another of pinky red rouge, and a slot for a brown eyebrow pencil. I gloated over them. Lastly, I discovered a little golden tube of lipstick.

How carefully I applied the cream to "deep-cleanse the pores." How briskly I rubbed it off "to promote a youthful glow." Then, more carefully than I had ever done anything before, I applied, ever so subtly, the rouge, the lipstick, and the eyebrow pencil.

The finished product was devastating. I looked in the mirror and fell in love, like Narcissus before me. I made plans to get up a half-hour earlier each morning so that I would have time to do a good job before school.

Also, I realized that this would

"Baby-care" is Beauty-care ·· use

run into money. I would have to see about more coupons—maybe from the neighbors—and then more quarters. It would never do to run out of these glamorous necessities.

It was like a movie entrance. When I came down the stairs, Grandma stood at the bottom. She took one look, raised her eyes to heaven and implored its Ruler, "Good Lord, what is that stuff on the child's face?" Receiving no answer from Him, she asked me, "What is that stuff?" But she waited for no answer from me, either. "Go wash yourself," she ordered grimly.

One look at her and I burst into tears. But even as I cried bitterly, I still found my way to the kitchen, where I began to ladle water from the stove's reservoir.

Nor was that all. "Where's the rest of it? Bring it here." It was no earthly good to evade or lie. I was convinced that Grandma had ESP—or I would have been convinced, if I had ever heard of it.

I fetched the box and Grandma disposed of it in an unbelievable way. We did not have garbage disposal in the country. The hogs obligingly took care of surplus food. Sometimes Grandpa took a collection of imperishables, like broken glass, tin cans, worn-out shoes and so forth, to the dump in a nearby city. But Grandma put all of my glamorous goodies straight into the kitchen stove, which was at its hottest in preparation for Saturday's baking.

Have you ever smelled cold cream cooking? Or rouge and powder? One smelled sweetly greasy. The other smelled dusty and scorched, like flour I once spilled on the stove, only sweeter. The cream jar cracked in a small explosion and its shards clinked inside the stove.

The odors permeated the house, and nothing could have been more nauseating. As the hours passed, Grandma's face grew grimmer and grimmer. Grandpa vowed that it gave him a headache, and he went to the village store for the afternoon. As for me, I was so disenchanted that Grandma had no further worries about having a "painted hussy" in her house for the next couple of years.

I shook my drying hair and took a long look at that little lady. She was barely 5 feet tall and her top weight was about 90 pounds. She had given birth to 11 children and raised 10 of them to maturity. She was a farm woman who had worked hard all her life and never had a luxury, used makeup or had a permanent. I knew she was in her late 60s, but there she stood, slim and straight and fresh-skinned. "Grandma," I said, "I hope someday I'll be as good-looking as you are." ❖

BARBARA BEL GEDDES, STAR OF STAGE, SCREEN, RADIO AND TV SELECTS
AVON COSMETICS AIDED BY MRS. EVELYN L. RYDEN, AVON REPRESENTATIVE

"It's so easy to choose Avon Cosmetics just right for your needs!"

Barbara Bel Geddes
Star of "The Moon Is Blue"

*"Avon 'Forever Spring' Cologne
is so refreshingly fragrant!"*
—Barbara Bel Geddes

"Selecting Avon Cosmetics best for your complexion needs is so convenient . . . with the Avon Representative, in your own home," says charming Barbara Bel Geddes. "And Avon Cosmetics are so fine in quality . . . so flattering in color tones . . . so delightfully scented!"

You, too, will be most pleased by the beauty benefits, convenience and economy of fine cosmetics chosen the Avon way. Your Avon Representative will help you. . . . Welcome her when she calls.

Avon COSMETICS

Hair Remedies

By Kathleen Peterson Talley

I remember when my neighbor's grandma would wash her little granddaughter's hair. She made a solution with vinegar and water, and poured that over her hair as a final rinse. She set her hair with this green goo from a bottle.

I think it was called Wave Set and was made by the Nestle Co. We were always tempted to put our fingers in the bottle when she was not looking. She also collected rainwater, heated it, and washed her hair with that.

I used to set my hair with these little rubber curlers that looked kind of like miniature champagne glasses. You would roll your hair around the stem part and then fasten the cap down.

I think we used those to make drop curls at the ends of long hair when we wore our hair in a long graduated length in the 1950s.

Sometimes we would mix up an egg and make a rinse to pour over freshly shampooed hair. It was good for your hair.

When I was little and for special occasions, my mother used to set my hair with rag curls. She would use pieces of cloth and wrap small amounts of hair up around the cloth and fasten it in a kind of knot, I think. It would be very bumpy to sleep on.

Oh, what a price was paid for beauty! Then she switched to large brown rubber curlers to curl my hair. I think these also came in pink, but for some reason she only used the brown ones, much to my dismay.

We ordered some stuff called Easy-Do from Meier and Frank department store in Portland in the 1950s. It was used as a setting lotion and was a milky white in color. We could hardly wait for it to get here. Finally it came. It was in a bottle and cost $1.50, which was a lot of money for us in those days.

It worked neat and you set your damp hair with it before putting the pins or curlers in your hair.

Seems our sets lasted longer, or we imagined and thought they did anyhow.

Prell shampoo was the first shampoo we bought. My mom was forever telling me, "Don't use too much when washing your hair as a little will go a long way."

Lustre-Creme shampoo in the blue and white jar was good also. You dipped into the jar like cold cream. It was a very nice shampoo to use and was endorsed by all of the Hollywood movie stars in the magazines. Their hair always looked so nice in the ads. Ours could too, we thought.

Little did our hair know what was in store for it in the years to come. It was about to be teased and then coaxed into the enormous beehives of the 1960s. If that wasn't enough, an ironing board was gotten out and it was then ironed straight as a stick and then parted down the middle.

Later, crimping irons were all the rage. Then cornrows came into fashion. The hair was plaited into small sections and then into cornrows.

If you got tired of washing your hair with water and shampoo, then a product called Mini-Poo was your answer. You applied the powdery substance to your dry hair—then brushed it out with a brush.

It was supposed to remove oil and grime, but all it did was make a big mess and you had to shampoo it out later anyway.

Hair products have come a long way since then, but I have enjoyed using all the products of yesteryear. ❖

Hollywood Glamour

FOR YOUR HAIR

LOVELY
BONITA GRANVILLE
Featured in Monogram's "SUSPENSE," a King Brothers Production

New Toni

WITH PRICELESS PINK LOTION

Holds the set longer than any other permanent

Ann's Toni was set today   **Roxie's Toni was set a week ago**

Imagine a permanent that holds the set for a whole week – without re-setting. That's New Toni with Priceless Pink lotion!

Never before a wave so lovely! So lively! So lasting!

You'll forget all other ideas about permanents the first time you use New Toni with Priceless Pink lotion. For it gives a soft, natural-looking wave that holds the set longer than any other permanent.

Never a lotion so wonderful! New Priceless Pink lotion curls more *completely*—yet is *kinder* to your hair! And that means a lovelier, livelier wave. Less re-setting. New freedom from the nightly chore of pin curls.

Take a tip from Ann and Roxie Shumaker— have a New Toni with Priceless Pink lotion today.

New Toni Refill $1.50

Toni makes you forget
your hair was ever straight!

Home Solutions

After World War I, more and women cut —or "bobbed"— their hair. Next came a succession of short, head-clinging styles inspired by film stars like the page boy of Greta Garbo and the peek-a-boo of Veronica Lake.

Short hair greatly increased the popularity of the permanent wave, but early permanents required heat, took 12 hours, and many times created a frizzy effect.

In the 1950s the invention of rollers for waving made possible very short, layered cuts. Now women could set their own hair at home.

Next came handheld blow-driers and even a home version of the salon drier.

The result: Most women made fewer visits to the beauty shop and had more home solutions for their hair. ❖

Below: Wrapped in a towel, a little girl is having her hair dried with a handheld hair dryer. The year was 1959. Photo by Chaloner Woods. Getty Images

Right: Multitasking was already on the rise by the early 1960s. English film glamour girl Barbara Roscoe is pictured in May 1963 at home in her kitchen cooking and reading while under the newest rage—the home hair dryer. Photo by John Pratt/Keystone Features. Getty Images

Early Curls

By Helen Keillor

Sixty-plus years ago, having a perm in a beauty salon was not the breeze it is today. I remember my first experience in this grown-up world of beauty.

In our small town, it took many nights of baby-sitting to accumulate enough money to go to the city for a long-awaited permanent wave. I was allowed to go alone, which was a great thrill. The hairdressing school (for that was all I could afford) was situated on the third floor of a walk-up building.

My long hair was wrapped and saturated with a terrible, eye-burning solution. I could scarcely breathe for the fumes, but I was happy.

The next step puzzled me, but I gladly did as I was asked, and sat under an umbrella-type monstrosity with each curl hooked up to a receptacle that fit over the curler. I was literally hung up by my hair. Then everyone left me and went about their business.

A few minutes later, with my head and eyes burning, I smelled smoke and noticed a stir of excitement. Then I heard the fire engine. My grown-up sophistication quickly abandoned me as I turned into a scared little girl. But I couldn't get away unless I scalped myself!

Quickly—although it seemed like it took a long time—a girl came to undo me. But before she was half-finished, a fireman came in and said all was well. There had been a small fire elsewhere in the building.

I left that beauty school many hours later with a head of wonderful curls.

Yesterday I got a beautiful, worry-free perm in just over an hour.

Things change in 60-plus years. ❖

The Original Curly Top

Early curls were made by an odd assortment of whiz-bang wonder predecessors. On the facing page at top are two examples of hair driers.

The Frankenstein-esque device at top right is the Nestles' permanent wave invention of 1910. Individual strands of hair were wound to the heat coils hanging from the device.

Women flocked to beauty salons for a headful of curls and thus liberated themselves from sleepless nights on rag rollers, all for the sake of beauty.

At left is a typical night stand for ladies in the Good Old Days. Note the curling iron that made curl touchups quicker and easier. Before electricity came to farms, a curling iron was hung in the globe of an oil-burning lantern.

Why the fuss for all those curls?

Americans were caught up in the fad brought on by America's sweetheart, Shirley Temple (right).

Shirley Temple

The difference
between this...→

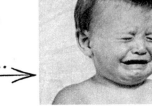

and this...↘

is
often
this...
→

Soft as Silk

At what point was it discovered that baby powders and baby oils were good for the beauty of adult skin?

To get the answer, you have to go back to the late 19th century. Johnson & Johnson was the one of the largest producers of surgical dressings in the world, pioneering the idea of antiseptic gauze for bandaging wounds.

The company also developed a plaster used for making casts for broken limbs. One of the main complaints about its plaster was that it caused skin irritation and rash.

In 1890, Fred Kilmer, a Johnson & Johnson employee, suggested that the company send patients containers of talc to sooth the irritated skin. Soon customers began asking for more of the scented powder. In 1893, the company began marketing it as Johnson's Baby Powder.

Soon an entire line of other baby products—not the least of which was Johnson's Baby Oil—was following the baby powder to store shelves.

The company produced a series of advertisements, proclaiming the new line of products as "Best for your baby, best for you."

By the late 1940s, women discovered that the products were, indeed, best for both mother and child. Soon Johnson & Johnson was selling more and more of its baby products to a new segment of the market.

It made the babies of the boom years happy—and left their mothers soft as silk, too. ❖

Hard as Nails

Even in the mid-1920s, women's etiquette books warned women against painting their nails with "garish colors."

This was just as nail polish was gaining ground in the market. The same year, Max Factor introduced the company's Supreme Nail Polish—actually a powder that was sprinkled on the nails and then buffed, shining them and giving some tint.

Various tints of red were the most popular in the 1920s and 1930s.

In 1932, the art of nail polishing took a giant leap forward when Revlon laboratories created polish based upon pigments rather than dyes. Not only was the new polish non-streaking, the process made it possible to create a variety of colors.

Revlon also promoted the fashion of matching lipstick and nail polish colors in the 1930s.

By 1938, pedicures and paint for toenails were growing in popularity.

In the 1940s, silver-screen actresses were the models for nail fashions. The nails of the 1920s and 1930s were more pointed; those of the 1940s were more rounded, *a la* Rita Hayworth.

In the early 1950s, it was much more fashionable to emphasize a woman's eyes than her lips and nails.

In 1959, Max Factor's Nail Enamel was introduced, and the next year the first false nails were introduced.

By the 1960s, with virtually every color of nail polish imaginable available, nail polish was no longer considered "garish." ❖

HYBRID MAGNOLIA

Fingertip Glory!

Your hands come to life,
as graceful and delicate as an exquisite flower . . .
when fingertips are done with glorious,
glamorous Dura-Gloss. Dura-Gloss, the polish of
perfection, is smooth to apply,
dries with speed, stays on for days.
At all cosmetic counters. 10¢ plus tax.

Something New
Dura-Gloss Nail Polish Dryer—
dries polish faster. Try it.
10¢ plus tax.

The DURA-GLOSS touch!

16 Exciting Shades

Dura-Gloss is the only nail polish that contains Chrystallyne
Copr. 1945, Lorr Laboratories, founded by E. T. Reynolds

A Little Dab'll Do Ya!

Men's personal grooming was moving up on the ladder of priorities by the 1950s. We were still a long way from the idea of men and women sharing styling salons, but the stronger sex was certainly becoming more conscious, particularly in the area of hair care.

Do you remember the Brylcreem jingle from the 1950s?

~

Brylcreem, a little dab'll do ya.
Brylcreem, you look so debonair.
Brylcreem, the gals will all pursue ya.
They love to get their fingers in your hair!
Brylcreem was created in 1929 at a chemical laboratory in Birmingham, England. It was the first mass-marketed hair-care product for men.

Even a "little dab" became too much for the "dry look" of the 1960s. In fact, Gillette came out with The Dry Look, a men's hair spray, and proclaimed in ads: "The wet head is dead! Long live The Dry Look!" ❖

Did you know?

The phrase "a little dab'll do ya" gave rise to a famous cartoon line. Fred Flintstone's "Yabba dabba doo!" came from the Brylcreem jingle.

With hair like this, you'll hear:

One man tells another
NOTHING CAN OUTSHAVE A REMINGTON

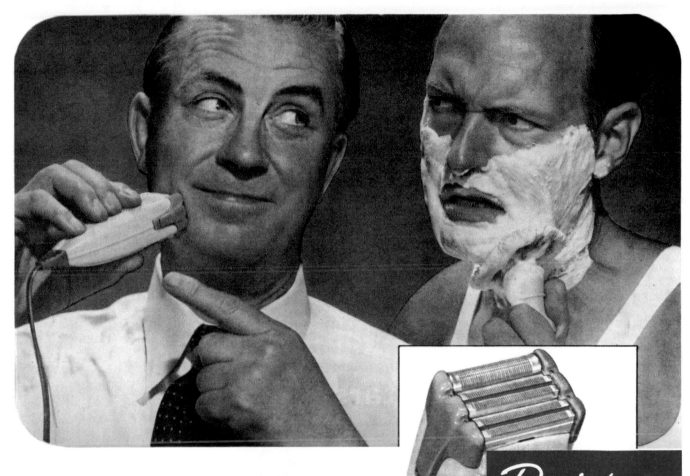

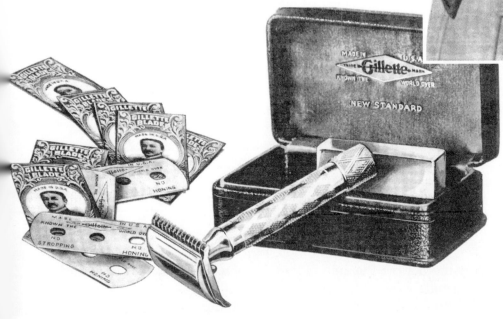

Shaving for most men even as late as the 1940s had changed little for decades. A straight razor (left) was still the utensil of choice. Then came the electric razor (above) and shaving was changed forever! The first electric razor was patented in 1928 by Jacob Schick (of Schick Shaver fame). The first electric shaver was on the general market by 1935.

An Evening in Paris

By D.J. Gaskin

As I held the small, cobalt-blue bottle in my unsteady hand, the coolness of the glass flat against my palm, I was transported from the oversized antique mall back to my grandmother's musty bedroom. I was staring at the same cobalt-blue bottle, displayed in front of the mirror on her stained-oak vanity. Then, moving forward in time a bit, I found myself facing my mother's mahogany dresser and, again, the same cobalt-blue bottle.

Now I held a replica of this precious glass—someone's memory. I wondered about the original owner, no doubt a woman like my mother, like my grandmother; a woman enticed by sweet scents. The smooth, rounded bottle still held the merest traces of scent, a liquid remnant in the bottom of the bottle. Evening in Paris.

Some acutely olfactory-oriented individuals swear that they can smell colors. Yellow smells of sun or summer flowers, warmth. Green evokes the scent of freshly mown grass. And the scent of autumn, to many, is clearly a red thing. This sweet perfume scent—this cobalt-bottled cologne—is what blue has always smelled like to me. And the sight of this bottle, only 4½ inches tall and just over 2 inches across its widest point, has always evoked memories of my grandmother and, most intimately, my mother.

I recall my mother in my teenage years before I left her, standing in front of her dresser, mesmerized over an identical bottle, undoubtedly recalling her own mother at every blue glance.

It was that connection—my mother's fascination with Evening in Paris—that compelled me to pursue this elegant vessel, and brought me, finally, to this place where I was holding the cool blueness in my hand once more. I had begun to believe I'd never find one; I was becoming convinced that none had been rescued from wherever used and empty bottles go.

After uncounted years, I noticed that my mother's own Evening in Paris bottle had disappeared from her dresser.

I had longed for this relic so fiercely; my search was heart-spurred, nothing less, certainly nothing more practical. I wanted—I *needed*—to give my mother her Evening in Paris, to give her back an old memory and the gentle scent of her own mother. For years I searched every antique shop in my path, only to come up empty-handed, until now.

Make Evening in Paris a part of you... Your perfume is as important to your charm as your perfect make-up, your shining hair, your exquisite clothes. Make *Evening in Paris* an always-present part of your loveliness. Remember, daytimes, evenings and always, *Evening in Paris* weaves a magic spell . . . and life can be much more exciting when you wear it!

Evening in Paris Perfume 75¢ to $12.50
Evening in Paris Eau de Cologne 65¢ to $1.50
Evening in Paris Face Powder $1.00
All Prices Plus Tax.

BOURJOIS

And now that I'd found this bottle—and with a drop of the scent still left from decades past—I realized, as tears welled up in my eyes, that it was too late. Mom had died just a few months earlier. I hadn't found that blue bottle soon enough. Now there was no address to which I could mail it; no one there to uncap the bottle, breathe in the scent of a yesterday long past, and call me to thank me through sentimental tears. It had taken too long.

still cologne in the bottle, about one-fifth or one-sixth full. Whose cologne? It moves the mind to wonder, to wander."

I can still see, behind my closed eyes, the image of my mother balancing her weight on one youthful hip in front of her dresser, unscrewing the silver cap and tipping the bottle for just a tiny dab of some of the last drops from what was once her mother's bottle, bringing her finger up to her nose to breathe in the scent before touching it to her neck, as she had watched her mother do.

I let the visions fade as I stood, nearly frozen in time, in that antique shop. I could keep this bit of nostalgia for $20, the tag said.

But I put the bottle back in its place, and continued down the aisle through this museum of antiques-for-the-taking, this collection of pieces of people's lives.

I moved past costume jewelry—silver birds and gold charms and other baubles—once treasured by women with names like Beatrice and Doris and Irene … maybe even names like Verna and Jean and Birdie, which were the names of my mother, her sister and their mother. And suddenly I knew what to do with the bottle.

I turned around and, in six long strides, reached my bottle. Holding it again, I walked up front and handed it to the cashier reluctantly, not wanting to let go of it again for even a moment.

I paid the $20 plus tax without bargaining, watched as it was wrapped in plain paper, carried it out in its tiny brown bag, brought it home with me, unwrapped it and set it in the middle of the kitchen table.

Editor Janice Tate remembers well her Evening in Paris days. These bottles are from her personal collection. The two at right are cologne bottles; the one at left is talcum. The small container (also pictured on page 118) was a cologne bottle for the purse.

Nowadays, I recently discovered, you can find one on the Internet through online antique merchants, and place a bid for one on eBay. A mere $45 on the Collecta-mania site buys you the 1-ounce size containing the precious scent that all girls (and their mothers) just had to have. It was the most popular scent of the era back in the 1940s and 1950s. One ad boasts, "There is

Then, with my favorite pen and a piece of old but elegant stationery I rarely use, I began to explain in a letter to my Aunt Jean the story of how I came upon this bottle, how I had meant it for my mother, and how I knew that she, my mother's sister, would appreciate it no less. ❖

Growing Up With Blue Waltz

By Jan Holden

Mom used to say that a girl becomes a lady when she starts spending her allowance on perfume instead of candy. I never gave it much thought until I got my first whiff of Blue Waltz perfume.

Let's see … I must have been about 10 years old when my older playmate, Judy, pulled the little heart-shaped bottle out of her purse and removed the powder-blue lid. Judy was a very popular girl, especially with the fellows, while I was everybody's kid sister. The "secret" to Judy's fascination, I surmised, must be the perfume she was wearing.

In 1959 I earned an allowance of $1 a week. It was amazing how far I could stretch that dollar at the local five-and-dime. Until I'd met Judy, however, the dollar nearly always was exchanged for gum and candy. Then, one afternoon, Judy handed me her bottle of Blue Waltz and told me to dab a bit on my wrists and behind my ears. Those were the proper places to put perfume, she advised, and I believed her.

The fragrance was so potent that it nearly knocked me over. It smelled a little like vanilla extract to my unsophisticated nose. When I mentioned that to Judy, she scoffed. "It's a poetic fragrance," she told me. And in 1959, I trusted Judy to be my aromatic adviser.

Looking back, I suppose that Blue Waltz, which sold for less than a dollar, must have been the perfume of choice for a lot of girls. It was affordable. It was easy to tuck into a purse. And it had a fragrance that seemed to grow more heady as the hours ticked away. I could still smell the aroma of vanilla extract (forgive me, Judy), even after my Saturday-night bath.

Of course, as I grew older and had a little more spending money, Blue Waltz sort of lost its appeal. The girls in high school were wearing Heaven Scent and White Shoulders. In fact, they were shopping at department stores and leaving the dime stores behind. Judy had moved to another town. I wondered if she was still wearing Blue Waltz.

I'll confess, until recently I hadn't given a thought to my first perfume, or to Mom's declaration that a girl becomes a lady when she starts buying fragrance. Then a pen pal mentioned she'd found a little store in her hometown that still carried Blue Waltz. Well, I just couldn't resist getting another sniff. Would the aroma still remind me of vanilla extract?

When the UPS man handed me the box, I opened it quickly. There, nestled in plastic foam peanuts, were a dozen bottles of Blue Waltz. How comforting to discover the same powder-blue lid!

And the fragrance? I'm not sure anymore. Maybe Judy was right. It is sort of "poetic." But maybe that's because it brought a tiny bit of yesterday to my present-day world. ❖

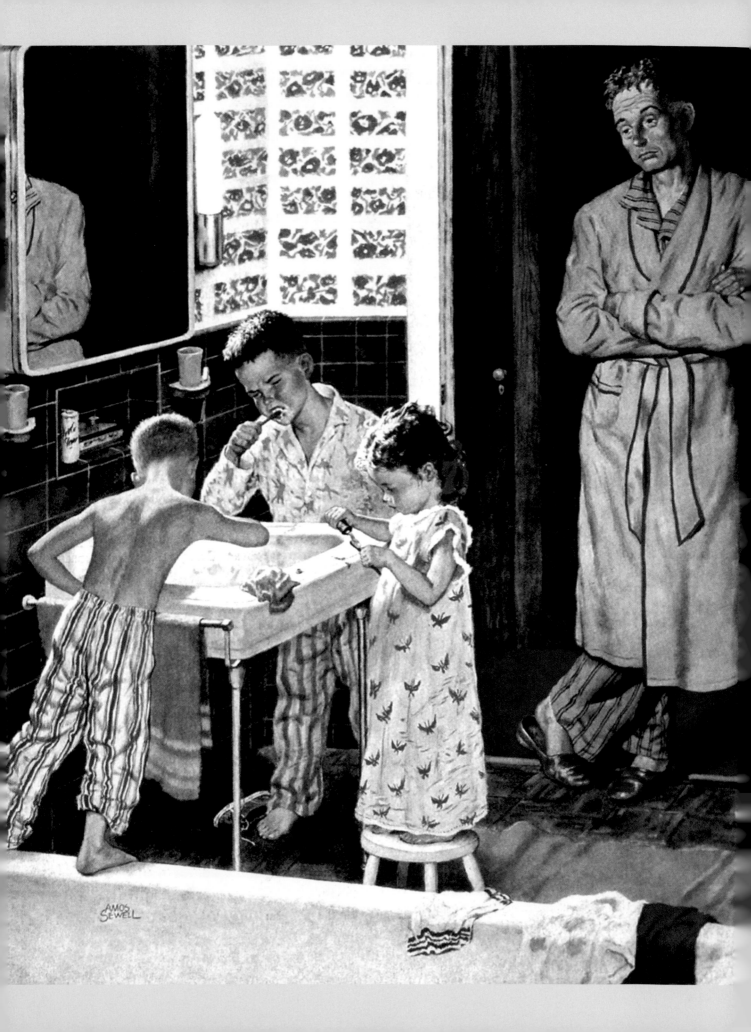

The Necessary Room

Chapter Six

I remember to this day the first time we were able to go to the tap and turn on a stream of water. It sounds so common today, but during the Dust Bowl days, running water was almost unheard of out in the country.

Then, after the droughts eased, Daddy and a couple of his brothers hand-dug a cistern and poured concrete walls. Gutters were added to the roof of our small home, draining rainwater into the cistern. An electric pump and pressure tank were added. When all the work was done, the water system was pressurized and we were all gathered in the brand-new bathroom, Daddy ceremoniously turned the new faucet on the sink and we danced gleefully as the water flowed.

At that moment, running water changed our lives forever. The changes were most evident in the "necessary room," as Mama euphemistically called the bathroom.

No longer did we have to make the trek down the pathway to the outhouse. No more fighting wasps and snakes in the summer. No more frozen backsides in the winter. Those changes were the most profound to a 10-year-old.

Baths could happen more than once a week— *drat!* Now when I took a bath, it was in fresh, warm water instead of water that had bathed three and was already rather cool. It still wasn't easy for Mama to get me into the bathtub, but when she did, it was a lot more pleasant experience.

Getting out of things was much tougher in general after indoor plumbing came along. Brushing our teeth is one example.

There were three children in our family: my older brother, Dennis, baby sister, Donna, and me. Before running water came into our lives, we often brushed our teeth, weather permitting, outside. It was easy to do a rather slipshod job. The routine changed after plumbing. Now when it came time for bed, we gathered around the sink in a well-lit bathroom with either Daddy or Mama wearily watching over the process. I like to think there were a few less cavities as a result.

Yes, the necessary room made a lot of changes in the life of this country kid. Begrudgingly, I must admit that almost all of them were changes for the better—even those involving soap and toothpaste!

—*Ken Tate*

Have a smooth-as-soft-water complexion

THE **CULLIGAN** WAY

Water, Water, Everywhere!

ater, water, everywhere—and not a drop to drink!" Do you remember that old saying? Well, for a lot of people back in the 1930s and 1940s, it was a saying that hit a little too close to home. We were immersed in an economic depression and a terrible drought gripped a large part of the country at the same time.

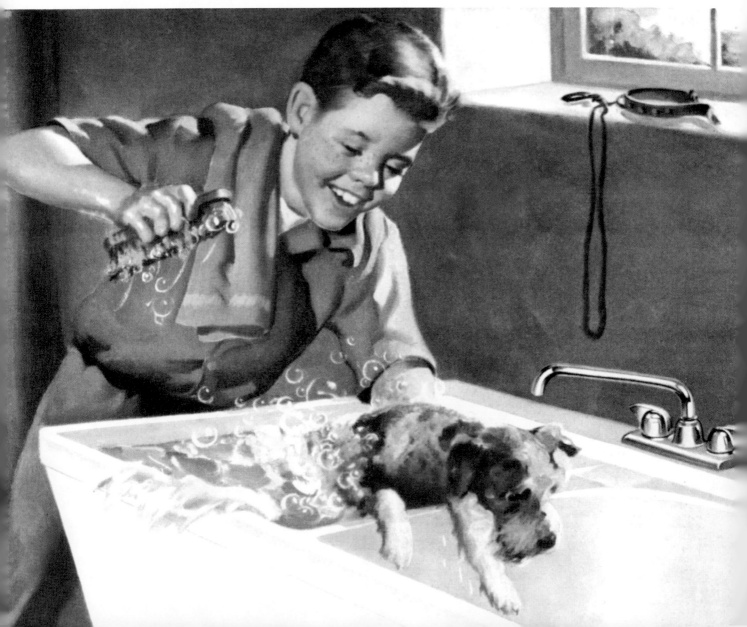

The first thing we needed to make our lives better was a reliable source of water.

By the time the second Dust Bowl of the 1950s hit, we were tapping into the deep aquifers of the earth and, despite the drought, we were able to enjoy "water, water, everywhere!"

Think of the changes having running water in the house meant.

The normal bathing routine for most families was the Saturday night bath. When you had to draw precious water from a spring, well or cistern by hand, a weekly bath was about all most families could handle.

One tub filled with water warmed on the wood-burning cookstove bathed the entire family. Father went first in the pecking order for the bath, followed by Mother and then the children in descending age.

That system even engendered a common phrase: "Don't throw out the baby with the bath water!" The baby was the last of the family to bathe in the same water, and the water became so dirty by the time Baby bathed that you had a hard time seeing her.

Wells and electric pumps in the country and pressurized water pipes in the city took care of our water problems. Now we could have electric and gas water heaters to deliver hot water right to the tub.

The tub itself moved from behind the heating stove in the living room. Now it was in the necessary room, providing a bit more privacy than the draped sheet divider of the old days.

For water that was too rich in minerals, companies like Culligan came along to provide rainwater-soft tap water.

Finally, we had plenty of water for those chores we could never do before. Washing the car, watering the grass and garden, bathing the pet dog—all those chores and many more were possible because we now had running water.

Finally there was water, water, everywhere—and plenty to drink, too! ❖

Tubs & Towels

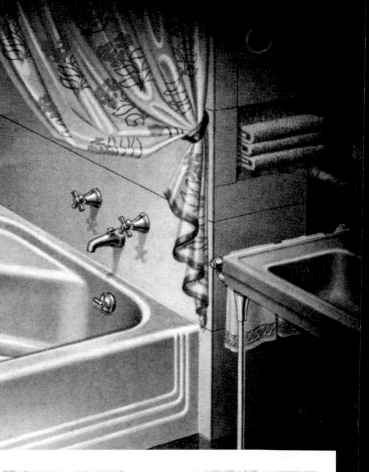

*T*he Saturday night bath was gone forever, thanks to tubs and towels! Now that running water was pretty much a universal commodity in the Western world, the necessary room included at least a bathtub—and usually a shower as well.

At first bathrooms were rather spartan

and severe. But soon, as the 1950s began to bloom, so did the walls, cabinets, shower curtains and towels. The bathroom became a place to decorate.

Decoration began with the towel rack. Cannon proclaimed that you could "Hang a rainbow in your bathroom!" Towels and washcloths reflected that rainbow beautifully. Not only was there a rainbow of colors for a discerning decorator to choose from, but Cannon also offered monogrammed towels. It was a personalized touch that many homemakers simply could not resist.

Color coordination also carried over to accessories. Shower curtains, bath mats, toilet covers—even soap and brushes—carried the color scheme throughout the necessary room.

Make your bathroom the safest room in the house—prettiest too!

Rubbermaid Houseware, already well known in the kitchen, came out with a line of bathroom accessory items to "Make your bathroom the safest room in the house—prettiest, too!"

Tubs and towels made bathtime a beautiful experience. Goodbye, galvanized washtub. Goodbye, Saturday night bath. And good riddance! ❖

Send for catalog showing complete line

Rubbermaid Houseware

The quality home-engineered brand that assures long life, resistance to soap, grease, heat and wear.

"You'll find Rubbermaid items wherever housewares are sold in the United States and Canada."

No More Tears

By Jessica Wyatt

*I*n the Good Old Days of the 1950s, when our children were small, keeping them clean was at the top of my priority list, like it was for most young mothers.

I suppose the toughest egg to crack was our son. Like most little boys his age, he *never* thought he was dirty and resisted all evidence to the contrary. When I was a girl in the days before running water, the once-a-week, Saturday night bath was a socially acceptable thing. I was bound and determined that it wouldn't be socially acceptable in *my* house.

New Beauty Miracle for Younger-Looking Hair!

Created by Procter & Gamble

NEW *Prell* leaves hair *'Radiantly Alive'*

...actually <u>more radiant</u> than cream or soap shampoos!

So, at least twice a week—more if the Lord gave me strength—I took him by twisted ear up the stairs to the bathroom and his date with a bar of soap and a tub. Cleanliness might be next to godliness, but it was also next to impossible with that boy!

I was so thankful for Ivory "it floats" soap. I don't know how I could have kept up with the soap and Kenny if it hadn't been for that.

I once read that Ivory was invented when a worker forgot to turn off his machine when he went to lunch. The machine accidentally beat air bubbles into the creamy soap solution and the result was a soap that floats.

However it came to be, it sure made the job of finding soap amidst a tub filled with soapy, dirty water and a squirming five-year-old easier.

The bath was no problem with our younger child—our daughter, Robin. I know some would call it stereotyping today, but she seemed to actually like to take a bath.

But I did have another problem. It was all I could do to get Robin to let me shampoo her hair. She hated to get water in her eyes, especially when it was mixed with the harsh soaps shampoos contained back in those days.

Then I heard of a new shampoo that came out—in 1955, I believe. It was Johnson's Baby Shampoo and the ads all claimed that it wouldn't burn or irritate the eyes. "No more tears," they promised.

I had used Johnson & Johnson's talcum powder and baby oil when the children were still in diapers, so I decided to give the new shampoo a try. It only cost about 60 cents, so what was there to lose?

I can't say that Robin looked as happy as the little girls in the shampoo ads I had seen in magazines, but she sure was a lot happier than with the adult brands. I even tried it myself!

The floating soap and no-more-tears shampoo completely cleaned up our act back in the Good Old Days. ❖

Lye Soap

Editor's Note: If you try this lye soap recipe at home, please note that lye is a toxic substance and should be handled with care. Lye soap was widely used in the Good Old Days. One advantage over commercial soap is that the natural glycerine remains in the mixture. It's also cheaper.

Use 2 quarts of melted grease from bacon drippings or scraps of fat meat. Stir in 1 cup of lye, dissolved in 1 quart of water. This will get hot during the mixing process. Allow to cool until lukewarm.

At once, add 1 cup of ammonia and 2 Tablespoons of borax dissolved in ½ cup of water. Stir for 5 minutes or until too stiff to handle. Put away to harden. It is best to let it set for four weeks. Nearly all soaps are better the older they get.

No more tears
from "soap in the eyes"

WON'T BURN or **IRRITATE** eyes!
- Lathers quickly even in hard water
- Rinses easily
- Pure, gentle, safe

New formula that **SHEENS** as it **CLEANS**

Johnson's BABY SHAMPOO
Johnson & Johnson

- Leaves hair glossy soft
- Easier to comb and manage
- Wonderful for all the family

59 and **98**¢

A Better Dental Plan

For centuries people have searched for ways to take care of their teeth. "Chewing sticks"—primitive toothpicks were in use as early as 3500 B.C. in Babylon. Toothpaste dates back to 500 B.C. in China and India. And the first toothbrush, also a Chinese invention, dates back to 1600 A.D.

Parents looking to enforce dental hygiene on millions of baby boom adolescents in the late 1940s and early 1950s, hoped that scientific discoveries would provide whiz-bang wonders to stamp out cavities.

The first big advances were made in toothbrushes themselves. Nylon replaced natural swine bristles in 1938. Brushes were developed with better handles, angled for easier and more effective brushing. Then came the first electric toothbrush, marketed in the United States by Squibb in 1960. General Electric introduced a rechargeable, cordless version the next year.

Brushes also became more colorful, sometimes even tied to cartoon characters or Western heroes in hopes of attracting young consumers.

We were becoming more mobile and busier all the time, so we were also looking for better ways to maintain a good dental plan on the run.

"Prevents decay, sweetens breath." That was the claim on the original package of Dentyne,

Here's a toothpaste for people who can't brush after every meal

JUST _ONE_ BRUSHING destroys decay– and odor-causing bacteria!

GLEEM with GL-70

invented by Franklin Canning, a New York City drugstore manager, in the early 1900s.

Canning's gum got its name from combining the words "dental" and "hygiene." Dentyne was bought by the country's leading gum manufacturer, American Chicle Co., in 1916.

Advertising campaigns in the 1950s and 1960s made Dentyne gum synonymous with fresh breath. The "Brush Your Breath With Dentyne" campaign of the 1970s still carries name recognition for the gum a quarter of a century later. ❖

"I'd like to meet that man..

THE ONE WHO CREATED THIS DELICIOUS DENTYNE"

"I'm sure he must be different and exciting . . . like the Dentyne flavor. And he must have high ideals, too, because Dentyne is really the finest kind of gum . . . quite in a class by itself. Have you noticed how much chewier it is? My dentist tells me it is very good for my teeth."

A long time ago people ate more chewy foods. And they had but little trouble with their teeth. Today we eat soft, tender foods. We chew less. And our mouth health suffers.

Dentyne supplies this necessary chewing exercise. It helps your mouth to cleanse itself. It strengthens and stimulates.

Most people—however—would chew Dentyne anyway just for its wonderful flavor. Its delightfully spicy, tempting goodness and the pleasant firmness of its "chew" make Dentyne the favorite chewing gum of thousands and thousands of intelligent people. You should try it today.

Chew delicious

KEEPS THE
MOUTH HEALTHY
KEEPS TEETH
WHITE . . .

DENTYNE CHEWING GUM
KEEPS THE TEETH WHITE

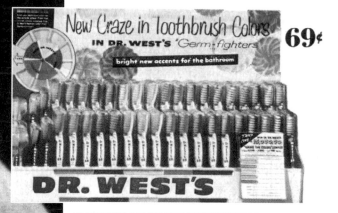

New Craze in Toothbrush Colors
69¢
IN DR. WEST'S 'Germ-fighters'
bright new accents for the bathroom
DR. WEST'S

Breathy Jingles

The Dentyne jingles of the 1970s are renowned as some of the most annoying—and most effective—of all time.

Here is one sample for you to remember them by:

They loved your dress,
They loved your hat,
But your breath could knock
Godzilla flat!
Brush your breath,
Brush your breath,
Brush your breath with Dentyne.
You love your plants and never frown,
But when you talk they all turn down!
Brush your breath,
Brush your breath,
Brush your breath with Dentyne.
That good-night kiss was some surprise
'Cause all she did was roll her eyes!
Brush your breath,
Brush your breath,
Brush your breath with Dentyne.

Burma-Shaving & Beyond

*T*he world of shaving had changed little in hundreds of years before the whiz-bang era. Men still whipped up a lather with a brush in a mug of some kind. A soap made by Burma-Shave (facing page) or Williams (below) provided the suds. They then used a straight razor of some kind to scrape the whiskers from their faces. Is it any wonder only

WILLIAMS Glider

A SPECIAL PREPARATION FOR SHAVING

FOR THE 1 MAN IN 7 WHO SHAVES DAILY

THE FINEST SHAVING INSTRUMENT OF ALL TIME

"one man in seven" shaved daily?

Then, beginning for most men in the late 1940s and early 1950s, the electric razor changed the shaving world forever. Companies like Schick and Remington were on the cutting edge of the new technology, but it wasn't just about the shaving. Lectric Shave was a pre-shave splash for men using new electric razors.

Aftershave lotions became more popular as well. "There's something about an Aqua Velva man," the ad proclaimed. The Aqua Velva man always got the girl—so a lot of men always got the Aqua Velva.

We've come a long way since the days of Burma-Shaving. Thanks to those new products, the ratio of men shaving daily as surely gone up as well! ❖

Sign of the (Passing) Times

When the kids of the 1940s and 1950s think of Burma-Shave, one of their best memories are those of the Burma-Shave signs along highways back in the Good Old Days.

It was refreshing to read the wit so cleverly mounted on these sets of five evenly spaced signs. These verses were erected along Highway 81 west of Belle Plaine, Kan.:

It's Not How Slow
Or Fast You Drive,
The Question Is
How You Arrive!
Burma-Shave

That She Could Cook
He Had His Doubts,
Until She Creamed
His Bristle Sprouts
Burma-Shave

Said Farmer Brown,
Who's Bald On Top,
"I Wish I Could
Rotate The Crop."
Burma-Shave

This one offered a humorous but solemn warning for all ages:

Drinking Drivers,
Nothing Worse,
They Put The Quart
Before The Hearse.
Burma-Shave

We miss those words of wit, but now we travel so fast that we could never read them. The slower pace of those days made it possible to go Burma-Shaving. ❖

The Throne Room

By J.G. White

Those who were born after 1940 are not as conscious of the convenience of a bathroom as those born before.

Today, if we don't have at least two bathrooms in the house, we think we are living in poverty. If there are only two people living in a house, a person can still soak in the tub for an hour or sit and read the *Reader's Digest* without being rushed out, if you have more than one bathroom.

I was 9 years old before we lived in a house with a bathroom.

Some years ago, when the television show featuring Desi and Lucy Arnaz was so popular, one episode featured Tennessee Ernie Ford, who went to visit them in New York.

After he had been in their apartment for some time, he left. He was back in a minute and left again by another door. He did it again and finally whispered into Desi's ear. Desi whispered into Ernie's ear. Ernie exclaimed, "In the house!"

Our early bathrooms were not the same as the toilet. The two functions were performed in separate facilities. When we took a bath, we went outside and got the tub and set it in the middle of the kitchen floor. If it was winter, we set it near the cookstove. After heating enough water in the teakettle, we took a bath.

Usually Charles took his bath, then James Lee, and I was last, all in the same water. After that, Mother scrubbed the kitchen floor with the water—and I mean *scrubbed* and not *mopped*. No need to be wasteful, especially if you had to make several trips to the well or water barrel or other water source. But there was no need to worry about scrubbing the floor or having an outhouse where we lived in Kent County.

There we lived in two tents with dirt floors, and the cedar trees were so thick that a person could hide himself real quick. The big problem there was the rattlesnakes that also hid in and around the brush and bushes.

Our toilet was a little outhouse, 50–100 feet or more from the back of the house. It measured about 4 by 5 feet, and was 6 or 7 feet tall.

A toilet is called an "outhouse," but all outhouses aren't necessarily toilets. An outhouse can be any kind of small building near the house or barns.

Often a smokehouse, which was larger than a toilet but still not very big, was fairly close to the house, and so was a tool shed.

Some toilets or outhouses were larger than others. Most of them were two-holers; that is, the bench or seat had two holes of comfortable size, side by side for fellowship. Some were three-holers, for even greater fellowship.

Usually the larger ones had a gable roof and were covered with car siding. They were more windproof than the little two-holers, which were

"*I want a gorgeous bathroom!*"

boxed up with 1 x 4-inch boards; the north wind and snow could easily circulate around and between them.

Bathroom tissue was either unknown or too expensive in those days, so we used whatever was convenient. The most convenient item was the Sears or Wards catalog (the outdated one, that is). Those who could afford to buy newspapers used them.

Most schools had two fairly large toilets—one for boys, one for girls—and they were separated by quite a distance.

Some schools had only one, and it was for the girls. The boys had to go into the bushes, if there were any bushes. That explains why there were usually two toilets at schools on the high plains of Texas.

One school that I know of had no outhouses at all. The boys went to the bushes on one side of the school and the girls went to the bushes on the other side.

Outhouses were favorite targets at Halloween. Big kids loved to turn them over. One guy said that he never turned them over; he and his friends just moved them back about 4 feet.

One man I knew evidently built his toilet in an area where the wind channeled down the hill, because the wind blew it over several times.

Finally he put a big post in the ground at each corner and anchored the toilet to them.

He had no more trouble with the wind, but one early morning, as he went out the back door, he saw that his toilet had burned down in the night.

They kept a candle out there to use when

it was dark. His teenage son had forgotten to extinguish the candle the night before.

My favorite story was told about an elderly woman I knew. The hinges had come off her family's toilet door, so when someone went to the toilet, he would just set the door in front of him, and when he left, he leaned the door to the side. You could tell if the toilet was in use by the position of the door.

One day, the lady went to use the outhouse. Since no one lived very close and those who came by seldom came close to the house, she just didn't place the door in front of her.

As she sat there, she became absorbed in the catalog and forgot where she was.

When she heard a horse trotting by, she looked up to see a neighbor, Mr. Hatchett, riding by. As she looked up, she said, "Good morning, Mr. Hatchett," and then returned her attention to the catalog. ❖

The Great TP Run

*T*oday few are left who remember the great bank run that closed so many financial facilities after the stock market crash of 1929. But many will remember the run on stores the morning of Dec. 20, 1973, that resulted in The Great Toilet Paper Shortage!

The run on toilet paper began as a joke by Johnny Carson on *The Tonight Show* the previous night. Johnny was delivering his monologue, which included a joke that began: "You know what's disappearing from the supermarket shelves? Toilet paper. There's an acute shortage of toilet paper in the United States."

The joke was based on a statement by Wisconsin Congressman Harold Froehlich, who claimed, "The United States may face a serious shortage of toilet tissue within a few months."

The power of suggestion was stronger than anyone could have suspected. The next morning word of the "shortage" spread like wildfire and consumers began buying up all the toilet paper they could find. TP began disappearing from supermarket shelves, confirming the shortage in the minds of millions. By noon most stores were completely out of stock.

Johnny tried to reel in the hysteria by apologizing and explaining that there was no shortage, but shelves remained empty, and the TP stampede continued.

Scott Paper officials appeared on newscasts, asking consumers to stay calm, and asserting that there was no shortage. The company even allowed news video of plants in full production, but it did little good.

Grocery shelves were restocked within about three weeks, and the "shortage" was over. Some say it was the only time in American history that panic-driven consumers actually created a major shortage. ❖

The ScotTissue Twins

Softie   Toughie

A Pair You'll Love

SOFTER THAN BEFORE, ScotTissue today gives you extra bathroom luxury and comfort. Yet it also has the strength so necessary for secure and thorough cleansing.

These *twin qualities—softness* and *toughness*—make Scot-Tissue an ideally balanced toilet tissue. Its extra softness is safe for baby's tender, sensitive skin . . . and its sturdy toughness resists tearing and shredding, even when moist —assuring immaculate protection.

And ScotTissue is economical. A roll a month for each member of the family is a normal supply. There's enough ScotTissue if everyone *shares* by keeping only a normal amount on hand.

Soft as old Linen

Scot Tissue

The absorbent soft white Toilet Tissue

3 for 25¢

1000 SHEETS

Scott Paper Company, Chester, Pa. U.S.A.

Ode to the Outdoor Privy

By Bonnie Speer

Recently I read that an elderly lady still used an outdoor toilet. She had never had the convenience of indoor plumbing and saw no reason to change her ways at this late date. Besides, she liked her outdoor toilet.

I can understand her feelings. Looking back to those days when I was a kid on the farm, there was something about an outdoor toilet that can never be matched by today's gleaming, tiled bathrooms. An outdoor toilet was one of the last bastions of privacy. It was a place where a kid could go and think for a while. It provided an excuse for getting out of doing the diner dishes when company came, or at least delaying the tedious job.

The toilet—or "privy," as some called it—was usually fitted with an old Sears & Roebuck catalog, or one from "Monkey Wards." Here one could sit and dream for a few minutes while looking at the pictures. (My husband claims that his family could tell when it was cotton-picking time because that's when they got down to the harness section.) Or one could just gaze out the open door at the distant fields, enjoying the sights and sounds of nature. How does that compare with today's tiled cubicles, where all there is to stare at are porcelain tubs and plastic flowers?

In the winter when it was cold, that trip down the well-worn path was taken in a hurry!

Of course, there were a few negatives to using the outdoor privy. In the winter when it was cold, that trip down the well-worn path was taken in a hurry! This was no time to linger and study the catalog.

Privies were often the home of lurking spiders. More than one person has been bitten while sitting there. I remember the day it happened to my father. A black widow spider nabbed him. We girls were shut out of the bedroom when the doctor came to call at our rural home (as doctors still did in those days).

My mother was so modest that she never did tell us girls until years later on which part of his anatomy my father had been bitten.

He was deathly sick for a while, but the old country doctor pulled him through.

The privies were also smelly. Today, all kinds of products are on the market to mask bathroom odors. Back in those days, a common method of purging the air (and spiders) was to set fire to a newspaper torch and thrust it down the toilet hole.

Most home toilets then had a single hole, but some had two or more. I suppose that was so one could have company when nature called, or so that things could be speeded up if one were in a hurry. Some of the toilets sported holes of varying sizes. I find this amusing as I look back, but they must have been custom-designed to fit those who lived there, like Papa Bear, Mama Bear and Baby Bear.

As a rule, the outdoor toilet was situated over a hole dug about 6 feet deep into the ground. When the hole filled with waste, the building was simply moved to another location and the first hole was covered with dirt.

These outdoor toilets were often the targets of Halloween pranks. A favorite trick was moving the toilet a few feet and waiting for some hapless victim to come out in the dark and step off into the hole at the end of the path.

One Halloween, when I was in the first grade at a rural Oklahoma school, my teacher, who boarded in a small cabin in a nearby neighbor's yard, came home to find her privy on the roof of her porch!

When I was young, my mother told a story about a child who had fallen into a privy and suffocated before they could get her out. *What a terrible way to go,* I thought. This story was in the back of my mind the day my small daughter came to the house and said, "Donna fa' down."

I knew instantly what she meant. At the time, we lived in a mobile home at the edge of a large peach orchard. An old privy was located in the orchard for the benefit of the seasonal workers. I knew the two girls, ages 1 and 2, had been playing around there. Sheer terror gripped me.

I woke my husband, who was working the night shift and sleeping days. Without waiting for him, I grabbed a long ladder and rushed to the privy. To this day I don't know how I thought I was going to get that big ladder down that little hole.

My husband came running behind me in his underwear. When I looked down that black hole, I saw nothing. My husband shoved me aside and took time for his eyes to adjust to the darkness. Then he saw her blond head. She was standing in the hole.

Quietly he coaxed her to lift her hands, and leaning down as far as he could, he pulled her straight up out of the hole. She must have fallen in feet first, for she was not soiled except on her feet. I was grateful that the toilet was old and little used, and I hugged my child in relief.

Outhouses were not found just in the rural world. Rows of outhouses were common in many parts of the country even into the middle of the 20th century. These steelmill workers' company houses and outhouses (above) were photographed in March 1936 in Birmingham, Ala., at the Republic Steel Company. Another row of houses showing backyard outhouses (below) was photographed in December 1935 in Cincinnati, Ohio. Photographs from the Farm Security Administration/Office of War Information photograph collection courtesy Library of Congress.

People often wonder how pioneers handled their toilet needs on their trek westward in wagon trains. Research reveals little. However, a few diaries relate that the women often clustered around each other, shielding each other with their long skirts, or holding up a blanket.

Men simply turned their backs to relieve themselves, or went off into the woods to do so in an unobtrusive manner—or some not so unobtrusive. One account relates how Gen. Andrew Jackson, who was bothered with the flu, draped his naked bottom over a fallen tree in plain view of his troops.

Following the Oklahoma Land Run of 1889, when 50,000 people converged upon the half-dozen town sites in the 200-million-acre reserve of virgin land, an enterprising settler in Guthrie found a way to get rich off the needs of people to relieve themselves.

After staking a town lot, he went down to the river and cut a quantity of leafy willow limbs. Returning to his lot, he dug a hole and erected the willows around it. He charged 10 cents a person for anyone using the hole, and made enough money to buy a blacksmith shop before some other fellows saw that he had a gold mine and went into competition, forcing him to lower his price to 5 cents.

Indians also had a sense of privacy, as did other early civilizations. Visit the 10th-century Viking village excavated in York, England, and you will see what looks like a large, woven basket with some guy peeping out over the rim. This was a forerunner of the later enclosed wooden squares. The use of privies, along with other poor sanitation habits, was believed to have contributed to the bubonic plague of London, which claimed the lives of 150,000 people between 1603–1605.

Generally, the 18th and 19th centuries in Europe was dominated by the pan closet, or jerry, or chamber pot, according to David Wallechinsky and Irving Wallace in *The People's Almanac*, *Vol.* 2. By 1800, many of these pots were elaborately decorated, even to the extent of placing the portrait of an archenemy in the target area. (Napoleon was a big hit in England.) After use, the contents of these pots were hidden in a commode or emptied.

At first, farmers collected the refuse, delighted to get the urban fertilizer. But as cities grew, the waste was generally collected by city "scavengers" and was dumped into large communal cesspits or the nearest river.

Just who invented the water closet is not known. Its origins go far back into history. One of the earliest indoor bathrooms has been found by archaeologists on Crete. According to Lawrence Wright, in his bathroom history *Clean and Decent*, King Minos included a water-supplied system in his great palace at Knossos. Cities in

The Outhouse Crescent

The crescent moon is widely associated with outhouses. But why? In *The Vanishing American Outhouse*, Ronald S. Barlow tells us that this symbol was originally intended for illiterate rustics. The moon, being a traditional female sign, indicated the woman's toilet, while a sun marked the man's. Because women's outhouses were better built, they usually lasted longer. Thus the crescent became the universal symbol for the outhouse.

the Indus Valley also had indoor, water-flushed bathrooms between 2500–1500 B.C. Except for the briefly used water closet of Elizabethan time, such engineering did not appear in England until the middle of the 18th century.

In 1850, Abigail Fillmore, wife of our 13th president, Millard Fillmore, said she was not moving into the White House until it was equipped with a Bible and bathtub. At her insistence, Congress appropriated funds for the White House's first library and indoor plumbing. (I wonder if there was a connection?)

The Rev. Henry Moule went down in history in 1860 when he set about trying to improve human sanitation habits by inventing what he called an "earth closet." This simple contraption consisted of nothing more than a wooden seat over a bucket and a hopper filled with dry earth, charcoal or ashes. The user pulled a handle to release dirt from the hopper into the bucket. The bucket could be emptied at intervals.

But the good reverend's name is not nearly so well known today as that of Thomas Crapper, who was reportedly the father of the flush toilet. British author Wallace Reyburn wrote an amusing biography about him in 1969 titled *Flushed With Pride*, but many historians believe this was a fictional story (though the Library of Congress files the title as if it were a serious historical treatise on the origin of the water closet).

It seems only logical that with the development of the water closet, *whoever* invented it, the creation of toilet paper would not be far behind (no pun intended). The first commercial product is credited to Joseph C. Gayetty of New York City in 1857. It was an unbleached, pearl-colored paper with Gayetty's name watermarked on each sheet. The paper sold at 500 sheets for 50 cents and was advertised as "Gayetty's medicated paper, a perfectly pure article for the toilet and the prevention of piles."

Like toilet paper, modern toilets themselves have come a long way in appearance. Even the name has been upgraded, for they are more often referred to in our country as "restrooms," or even more delicately, as "powder rooms." Seldom is an outdoor privy seen anymore, except for those smelly portable potties hauled around to construction sites and outdoor events.

This passing of the outhouse has been much lamented in books and poems, including those by such luminaries as Robert S. Service. These buildings represented a way of life that is no more, and a more leisurely era when the world seemed not so complicated. In looking back, I can quite understand that elderly lady's reluctance to give up her outdoor toilet. ❖

The Day the Privy Blew Up

By Melody Miller

Everyone in the Good Old Days had "a little house out back" that served its purpose when nature called. The following event took place on a small farm south of Edison, Neb., back in the early 1930s.

One day, the farmer's wife was cleaning some clothes with naphtha gas. There were no dry-cleaning facilities then, so if a garment needed to be spotted or cleaned, it was washed with naphtha gas and hung to dry. This gas was also used in gas lanterns.

After cleaning a few garments, she wondered what to do with the gas. Back then, when you didn't know what to do with such things, they were dumped down the outhouse hole—and that's exactly what she did with her bucket of naphtha gas. Soon thereafter, her husband came home and proceeded to the outhouse.

Now, there was one thing that the farmer enjoyed doing, and that was smoking his pipe while sitting on the throne in the outhouse. He took his pipe out of his pocket and carefully filled the bowl with tobacco.

He took a stick match from his overalls pocket, struck the match and lit the tobacco. Taking a few deep draws on the pipe, he relaxed and thought about his accomplishments of the day—and then he dropped the match into the other hole of the outhouse.

Boom! The match, still lit, ignited the fumes and the naphtha gas, and he suffered a flash burn on his posterior. He stumbled out of the outhouse, hitching up his pants as he ran, and stood watching in amazement as the old outhouse burned to the ground.

After the farmer's posterior healed and a new outhouse was erected, there were plenty of laughs and jokes made about his experience. But it sure wasn't funny to the farmer at the time! ❖

The Great Outdoors

Chapter Seven

All of the whiz-bang wonders that made our homes so exciting back in the Good Old Days still weren't enough to keep us indoors all of the time. There was plenty for a family to enjoy together beyond the doors and walls in the great outdoors. It didn't matter if the outdoors was several hundred acres on a farm, or just a half-grass, half-concrete front yard in Suburbia, we could always find something to do as a family.

Television had not yet dulled the imagination of our youth. We could play for hours with our toy cars, or string a tin-can walkie-talkie set between bedroom and treehouse. Family cookouts were a popular way to spend summer evenings and often the pungent aroma of barbecue on the grill was overpowered only by the whoops of kids joyously celebrating simply being alive.

I don't know if they had robbed the lawn mower motor for the go-cart, but I wouldn't be surprised if they had.

I remember a scene from the great outdoors I witnessed one autumn afternoon in a Kansas City suburb, a scene punctuated by the age-old need of youngsters and not-so-youngsters alike to get outside the confining walls of their homes.

I was visiting an aging aunt and was passing a row of homes near Mission, Kan., when I saw a family working on a go-cart project together. It reminded me of the painting by Thornton Utz on the facing page, first published on the cover of the *Saturday Evening Post* in 1958.

The father and his sons had strewn go-cart parts all over the driveway. The family car was parked on the lawn in obvious deferral to the importance of the project underway. The garage door stood open, but no mother would dare ask father or sons to move parts and tools to allow passage.

I don't know if they had robbed the lawn mower motor for the go-cart, but I wouldn't be surprised if they had.

Front yards and back yards were where our families became cemented together. The barbecue grill, the wading pool, the jungle gym and the croquet set all pulled us together for a few hours each week, and our families, communities and nation were stronger for it.

The great outdoors didn't have to be the wilderness of the Wild West. It didn't need to be anything grander than the small patch of grass that was our yard back in the Good Old Days.

—Ken Tate

Grooming the Lawn

By Ken Tate

Every year after the passing of the spring equinox, as I watch days lengthen and the brown of winter succumb to the green of another luscious spring, I face with absolute resignation the inevitability of another season spent grooming the lawn.

In some regards I loathe the task of mowing grass. My dear wife, Janice, would tell you that I grumble all the way down to the barn, where I store the lawn mower through the winter. I mumble my way through the pulling and cleaning of the spark plug, the draining and refilling of the oil, the filing of the blade to razor sharpness.

Some of the whys behind my aversion to cutting the grass date back to my youth. One of my childhood chores was to cut Grandma's grass, and her grass seemed to grow as if there were fertilizer in those April showers.

Then there was our mower. No gas-powered, two-stroke, internal combustion mower, riding or otherwise. No, I guess Mama and Daddy figured they had to fuel me up three times a day, so they might as well find out how many yards per gallon I got. The only power for that old reel mower was whatever power I

Three generations of tools for grooming the lawn. Left: A boy mows the family lawn in 1945. This is the type of manually powered reel mower mentioned in the story. Photo by Lambert, Getty Images. *The first reel mower in the United States was patented in 1868. Some early reel mowers were designed to be pulled by a horse, wearing leather booties to prevent lawn damage. Right: By the spring of 1950, companies like Reo Motors had added a motor to the reel mower, giving the whirling blades power. Top right: Rotary push mowers followed, but by 1959 the riding lawn mower was becoming increasingly popular for larger suburban lawns.*

generated. The more *umph!* I put behind pushes and thrusts, the faster the blades whirred, throwing clippings high enough to catch in the breeze and scatter on my shoe tops.

I had to make sure those blades stayed sharp and that the reel mechanism was well oiled, or the job just got tougher. And Mama didn't have to tell me twice that it was time to cut the grass at Grandma's because an extra couple of springtime days of growth made the blades of grass tougher than the blades on my not-too-trusty mower—or at least that's the way it seemed.

But then, after the job was done, Grandma invited me in for some buttermilk and corn bread and we sat on the porch while she praised the smooth carpet that resulted from a hard afternoon of work.

A teenager demonstrates his novel method of keeping cool while mowing the lawn in 1966. He is using his mother's umbrella strapped to his back. The photograph was taken in Miami, Fla., where keeping cool in the tropical heat isn't always easy. Photo by Alan Band/Fox Photos, Getty Images.

Then she bragged incessantly on me to Mama and Daddy. I always asked her not to, but … well, you know grandmothers.

Nowadays it's almost impossible to find a neighbor boy to hire to cut our lawn.

And, if we find one, he wants more money for one cutting than this old skinflint wants to pay.

Yes, I grumble when I first get out the mower in the spring and begin to think of another season of grooming the lawn.

But the truth is, I grumble because that's my nature.

The truth also is that I secretly enjoy pushing a mower in gradually smaller rectangles until the lawn is smooth.

So, I push on, greening up my sneakers with the trimmed blades of April.

When I'm done I'll sit on the bench to the south of the old home place and absorb the sun's warmth.

Maybe Janice will bring out corn bread and buttermilk—just like Grandma did when I groomed her lawn back in the Good Old Days. ❖

The Reel Lawn Mower

By Fred J. Kane

Today, kids still mow lawns at home as one of their weekly chores. Weekends, you can hear the lawn mowers running in the neighborhood. Some kids cut their neighbors' yards to earn spending money.

Today, kids use their parents' gas- or electric-powered lawn mower for this task. How about when you were a kid and the lawn mowers were propelled by hand?

Every once in a while you will travel through a section of town where building lots are small, and you will hear the *clickety-clack, clickety-clack* of the push-type lawn mower. It is correctly called a "reel mower." The reel mower was invented in 1830 in Great Britain. Country gentlemen used the reel mower as an exercise device.

The reel mower has curved blades that rotate between two wheels. Also, there are two half-round pieces of metal attached to the mower and the wooden handle.

At the end of the wooden handle is a T-bar that the operator grasped. Usually you pushed the mower in a straight line. It didn't have a steering wheel. Also, this mower used no power other than manpower.

Let me take you on a sentimental historical trip through time with the push-type lawn mower. Remember when a small piece of wood or a twig caught between the guide bar and the blade? Then the mower stopped abruptly and your belly felt the jab of the T-bar.

How did you remove it? The blades wouldn't turn because the twig was jammed between the bar and the blade. What did you do? You gave the curved blade a back-slap kick so it would release the wedged piece of material, or you bent to turn the blade backward. Then you could continue to mow the lawn.

In 1896, the average American family paid the outrageous price of $2.20–$4.75 for a reel mower. That year, the American Lawn Mower Company sold 4,000 reel mowers. During the war years of the 1940s, only reel mowers were used to cut the lawns in the good old United States. Retail sales of reel mowers jumped to 200,000 in 1945.

Do you remember the school custodian or the caretakers of large lots pulling their reel mowers behind a tractor? Sometimes the mowers were two abreast.

Imagine not having to push the mowers. Boy! What an easy life.

How about the man who rode his specially rigged bicycle through the neighborhood sharpening scissors, knives and mower blades?

Around 1953, increased sales of powered mowers contributed to the downfall of reel mower manufacturers and many smaller companies failed.

Then, when the price of land skyrocketed in the early 1980s, lot sizes became smaller and the demand for reel mowers became greater. From 1985–1991, reel mower sales soared to 150,000 units per year.

Today, because of environmental awareness and stiff air emission regulations and yard waste rules imposed and enforced by the Environmental Protection Agency, sales of reel mowers have peaked at 250,000. Today, a reel mower costs $75–$100.

When you drive around, look carefully; you may see a youngster making some spending money mowing lawns. And if you listen carefully, you may even hear the *clickety-clack* of a push mower in your neighborhood. Then you can remember making some spending money mowing lawns with a reel mower in the Good Old Days. ❖

Backyard Barbecues & Other Fun

*T*he boom years of the 1950s was not just about babies. We also had a booming economy, and with it came more leisure time and more ways to spend it.

Beginning in the days after World War I, there was a major population movement from rural areas of the country to cities. That movement continued until after World War II.

Then the move was from the city to the suburbs, the sprawling territories caught between city and country. Homes were larger and most

had back yards to provide space for growing families. Result: the birth of the backyard barbecues and other fun.

The back yard was a wonderful place to gather the family. We purchased canvas-stripped lawn furniture, picnic tables and barbecue grills.

Fathers who had never cooked a meal in their lives became experts in basting, marinating and searing. Some even went so far as to wear "Kiss the Cook" aprons!

Family games made up a big part of the backyard fun. Croquet, badminton, horseshoes and volleyball were games we could play together as a family.

Remember lawn darts? It was a popular lawn game for years until the federal government banned it for safety reasons in 1988. It remains a popular game in England even today.

After we had our fill of barbecue and tired ourselves out on games, backyard fun was far from over. On special occasions homemade ice cream was shoveled out of the freezer to the delight of kids young and old.

By the 1950s there were ice-cream freezers with mounted electric motors. The job of cranking out the dessert was easier, but maybe a little less satisfying than when it was accomplished using the hand-cranked model.

Vanilla was the easiest flavor to make, but it wasn't the only one. We added strawberries, cherries and blackberries, or topped the vanilla ice cream with nuts and chocolate syrup.

Did You Know?

The plastic pink flamingo lawn ornament that became ubiquitous in the late 1950s and early 1960s was invented by Don Featherstone of Massachusetts in 1957.

The Baby Boom was a great time for backyard barbecues. It was an economical way to prepare a special meal and also brought the family together on a summer evening. Left: Here a young couple barbecues in their suburban back yard in 1953. Their oldest son plays on the swing set in the background. Photo by Gordon Parks. Time Life Pictures/Getty Images.

Swing sets and jungle gyms were very popular for parents with youngsters. Facing page: A baby climbs on a jungle gym ladder in 1955. Photo by Harold M. Lambert/Lambert/Getty Images.

Maybe the variety didn't match Baskin-Robbins, but it sure was good on a hot summer day.

Hot summer days also called for the other standard of the great American back yard: the wading pool. There the kids (and sometimes the parents, too) could cool off after a wonderful day of games, food and fun.

Some families in the affluent 1950s even went so far as to build a backyard swimming pool. You always knew which home had one of those. It was the one with the steady stream of kids on sweltering days.

Yes, backyard barbecues and other fun got us out of the house and into the great outdoors back in the Good Old Days. ❖

Mama & Her Brownie

By Ethel Weehunt

As she recorded family history with her Brownie Box 616 camera, she was something of a photographic genius.

None of her work was so important but that she couldn't drop it to grab her Brownie and snap a photograph to include in the pictorial history of her folks and farm. This was Mama's hobby.

Her eye was quick to see a good picture. With a triggered snap, she could capture in black and white the persons and actions that were relative to family history. After the snap, she carefully rolled up the film. The number of the next shot showed in a small, round, glass-covered hole on top of the camera.

Mama seemed to have an instinctive ability to judge how a scene would look when reduced to the size of a snapshot.

To most favorably depict her subject, she could choose the better of two positions for holding the camera.

The horizontal position was best when several people or objects were gathered. The vertical was preferable for tall trees, skyscrapers and giraffes. Mama's Brownie captured everything—the tall and short, wide and narrow.

Now, years later, when we see what Mama saw through the Brownie 616, it all comes back. We again know the Good Old Days; we see the laughter and tears. The farm animals come to life again. We hear the horses crunching corn or oats from their feed boxes. We remember how they worked as hard as we did.

We again hear the voices of all the people of the farm and we remember their peculiarities and the distinguishing personalities that made them individuals.

And again we see Mama, Brownie in hand. We hear her calling, "Wait! Wait! I want to get your picture!" as she spies some person, animal or action that she believes will make a good photograph.

Thanks to Mama and her Brownie, we have a pictorial history that takes us back to the happy days down on the farm. ❖

Left: One of the photographs from Mama and her Brownie. I am pictured pitching hay in the late 1920s. Above: This Brownie with a foldable bellows lens was popular in 1905.

Lights! Camera! Action!

The Brownie camera may have been fine for the old days, but the whiz-bang era demanded something new and exciting. It came in the form of home movies—and prints and slides would never be the same again!

Remember the first time you wound the 8-millimeter celluloid from the film reel, threading it past the sprockets on each side of the lens opening and over to the take-up reel? Lights were doused and the projector flickered to life.

There, on a cheap imitation of the silver screen at the downtown theater, the events of our lives jumped out of the projector. The action was jerky and, of course, there was no sound. But Charlie Chaplin started out in silent films, so we could, too!

Dozens of companies jumped on the home movie market. Yashica (left), Eastman Kodak (below) and Keystone (facing page) were just a few of those scratching the itch consumers had for making their own living record of new babies, birthdays, holidays and marriages.

It was almost three decades before the magnetic video tape again redefined home movies. But the magic of those first flickering images from the whiz-bang years would stay with us forever. ❖

Puttering About the Garage

By Ken Tate

I'm a great putterer. My dear wife, Janice, says so, and she knows me better than anyone. I putter around the garage. I putter around the barn. I putter around the toolshed. I putter around most anything that looks like it needs to be puttered around.

Puttering is an art that should be on the endangered species list—something seemingly doomed to extinction by a too-mobile society that has no room to move all of the accumulations of life. Modern houses don't have attics—they have crawl spaces. Puttering space is usually reduced to the garage, and the things you might putter with are routinely disposed of in the perennial cleaning out of the garage.

Whenever I get a bit too melancholy, stir crazy or just too ornery to have around the house, Janice fixes it by suggesting, "Why don't you go out and putter around awhile?" She knows the psychological value of a good puttering session. It puts things in perspective. There is something about examining minutia that puts big things in order.

Once I asked Janice why she—and most women like her—don't putter. She retorted that women putter about the kitchen, putter with their knitting and crocheting, putter with their flowers. Men, she said, just refuse to recognize that as part of the art of puttering.

I grew up in hard times. There is something about not having much that makes you hold onto everything you do have. I have stored away dozens—if not hundreds—of relics of my childhood. Not that I'm sentimental, you understand. It's just that I never know when I might need that old rotten piece of hemp with which Daddy taught me to rope—first fence posts and then calves.

I have every nail and board left over from the last renovation of the old family home. I have every extra screw, nut and bolt that has ever been included in packages of pantry shelves, pieces of office furniture or new tractor parts. Whenever I tuned up our now-antique pickup, I always kept the old spark plugs and points, figuring I might need a spare set along the road someday. Much of this now inhabits a side shed in our barn—a musty old place near and dear to my heart.

I have said that my side shed is the equivalent to Janice's button box, where she rummages for the perfect button or snap for her latest project. She, of course, points out that her button box fits neatly in a drawer in her sewing cabinet, while my side shed looks like … well, you get the picture.

Yes, I like to putter. And I'm blessed with having lived in the same place long enough to have plenty of places to putter. Just talking about it makes me want to go and see what I can find. Janice wanted a whatnot shelf for the bedroom, and I think I know right where I can get the board and wood screws for it.

It's a good thing I held onto all that junk. Otherwise today I'd be headed for the store instead of using it up. ❖

Auto Magic

Puttering about the garage during those whiz-bang years really reminded us how much things had changed since the end of the Great Depression.

A campaign ad for Herbert Hoover's 1928 was the genesis for the promise of "a chicken in every pot and a car in every garage." That dream didn't materialize for nearly 30 years for most Americans. By the boom years of the 1950s, however, most garages (or yards, if you didn't have a garage) included a car.

The cars themselves were becoming whiz-bang wonders in their own right, too.

Push-button radios gave us tunes for the open road. The new Philco radios (left) even boasted a foot control so your hands never left the wheel.

Air-conditioned cars like the cool Chrysler (above left), were on the market by the mid-1950s.

Good economic times meant cars were relatively more affordable. That brought about another new phenomenon: the two-car family. In turn, that meant more and more women were enjoying the freedom of auto magic.

The Price to Go

With the escalating prices of gasoline in recent years, it might be instructive to look at comparisons from the whiz-bang year of 1954.

The American Petroleum Institute published an advertisement (right) that compared the price of gasoline in real-world terms: how long it took the average worker to earn enough to purchase a gallon. The caption for the ad reads:

"Today's gasoline is a real bargain. Comparing the number of minutes of work needed to buy a gallon of gasoline in 1925 as against 1954 illustrates sharp decline of gasoline's actual cost when compared to income.

"This is even more remarkable when you consider that these figures include gasoline taxes, which are up over 250% since 1925."

The statistics were based upon the average hourly earnings of American production and manufacturing workers reported to the federal government in1925 and 1954.

Index of Illustrations

This index includes the source of all illustrations used in this book, with the exception of those identified in caption material on the page on which they appeared. Except where noted, all illustrations are from the House of White Birches nostalgia archives.